Is Forgiveness Possible?

Joan Mueller, O.S.F.

A Liturgical Press Book

THE LITURGICAL PRESS
Collegeville, Minnesota

Cover design by Greg Becker.

1   2   3   4   5   6   7   8   9

Library of Congress Cataloging-in-Publication Data

Mueller, Joan, 1956–
    Is forgiveness possible? / Joan Mueller.
        p.   cm.
    Includes bibliographical references and index.
    ISBN 0-8146-2470-7
    1. Forgiveness—Religious aspects—Christianity—Biblical teaching.   2. Bible.   N.T.   Luke—Criticism, interpretation, etc. 3. Bible.   N.T.   Acts—Criticism, interpretation, etc. 4. Forgiveness—Religious aspects—Christianity.   5. Pastoral psychology.   I. Title.
    BS2589.6.F6M84   1998
    234'.5—dc21   97-20142
                                                              CIP

Contents

Veni Sancte Spiritus

INTRODUCTION

Toward a Contemporary Theology of Forgiveness

Forgiveness is a popular contemporary theme. Therapeutic researchers are spending significant sums delving into the benefits of forgiveness therapies. Forgiveness and reconciliation processes are being advocated by church activists in violence-ridden neighborhoods. Christian forgiveness and reconciliation are being promoted as political strategies for healing wounds in areas such as Northern Ireland and South Africa. In all these instances, Christian forgiveness is said to be the wellspring for the therapy, the activism, or the politics in question.

The systematic theologian reads this press and wonders: What is the nature of the forgiveness being talked about? If the forgiveness is Christian forgiveness, what is the source of its theology? Is its theology rooted in Scripture and tradition? What is the process of this forgiveness? Is this process rooted in Christian Scripture and tradition? What is the goal of Christian forgiveness? If it is reconciliation, what is the nature of this reconciliation? Can humans effect reconciliation? What is God's role in the forgiveness/reconciliation process? Is the operative theology of reconciliation rooted in Christian Scripture and tradition?

These are not idle questions. The tendency to use religion and religious terminology to advance self-serving ideologies has long afflicted Christian cultures. The fact that good, even exemplary people might be promoting these theologies does

1

not necessarily mean that the theology is solid. Without a solid theological base, people who are already vulnerable will only suffer more. Christian leaders need to reflect upon the source of their theology, not merely as an intellectual exercise, but as a way to serve their people. In situations of violence, there is little room for another well-intentioned mistake.

Finding models in the Christian tradition for theologies of forgiveness is not a simple task. Much of what exists addresses past ruptures in the Christian community and revolves around sacramental and legal paradigms. The contemporary situation, however, rarely revolves around a single Christian denomination, but includes Christians with differing theologies, as well as non-Christians.

The human realization that war, even holy war, could bring about the complete destruction of humanity is recent. The imperative to forgive in the atomic age is truly a human imperative and not just a Christian maxim. Christianity has the potential to bring much to contemporary forgiveness discussions. In doing so, the theologian needs assurance that the Christian theology being purported is rooted in Scripture and tradition.

This study is a preliminary attempt to catalyze contemporary theological discussion concerning the concepts of forgiveness and reconciliation. In doing so, its purpose is driven not by specious academic wanderings but by human need. If Christian therapists are suggesting forgiveness therapies to victims of rape, this therapy needs to be grounded in true Christian theology. If Christian activists are talking about reconciliation in gang-infested neighborhoods, gang members will quickly discern whether their talk is smoke or wisdom. If peacemakers are treading into countries suffering from the aftermath of ethnic cleansing, they need to be secure in their own source of peace. Charity is noble, but especially in limit situations charity that is not grounded in truth is dangerous.

Wanting to stay close to both Christian tradition and to contemporary forgiveness dilemmas, I choose to format this text in terms of a dialogue. From the tradition, I will focus upon the prayer of forgiveness in Lucan literature. From contemporary experience, I will engage the field of pastoral counseling.

Considering the need for this type of study in the contemporary world, this dialogue is a humble beginning. My hope is that it might provide a paradigm and impetus for further studies.

The first chapter introduces the dialogue partners. It begins by presenting a review of questions that arise in the context of contemporary pastoral forgiveness dilemmas. It then introduces a description of the term "the Lucan prayer of forgiveness" as it is used in this study.

In studying the Lucan prayer of forgiveness, certain textual and theological issues must be examined. Chapter 2 deals with these foundations. First to be explored is the place of prayer and the theology of prayer within the Lucan corpus. Second, biblical exegetes have debated the manuscript evidence concerning the prayer of forgiveness in the Gospel of Luke. In order to claim the discussion of the prayer of forgiveness as authentic Lucan theology, a review of this debate is included. Third, because the prayer of forgiveness requires of the Christian supreme faith in the fidelity of God, this theme as it appears in the Lucan literature is explored. Finally, the prayer of forgiveness is discussed within the passion narratives of Jesus and Stephen.

The third chapter explores the process of the Lucan prayer of forgiveness by means of three dynamics. The first dynamic, the prayer itself, includes calling upon God in order that God might forgive the persecutor, and excusing the oppressor on the grounds of ignorance. The second dynamic requires the handing over of the spirit of the victim into the hands of God. The third dynamic is the response of God to the victim's faith.

The contributions of pastoral theology also need careful consideration. Because the circumstances of forgiveness dilemmas reported by contemporary Christians seeking pastoral assistance differ from the predicaments of Jesus and Stephen, the Lucan paradigm cannot be uncritically applied. In order to assist those coming to them with forgiveness issues, pastoral theologians listen to contemporary expressions of these issues and reflect on them in light of the Christian tradition. As a fruit of their reflection, a number of theologians have proposed pastoral forgiveness theories. The theological foundations of five of these pastoral theories are examined in

Chapter 4 by means of three questions: (1) What is Christian forgiveness? (2) How does the Christian forgive? and (3) What is the relationship between forgiveness and reconciliation? Literature was chosen for this chapter on the basis of the authors' creative contributions and on frequent citings in professional literature.

Chapter 5 facilitates the dialogue between the Lucan prayer of forgiveness and contemporary pastoral forgiveness theory. The chapter addresses the questions raised in Chapter 4 and critiques pastoral answers to these questions in light of the Lucan prayer of forgiveness. The purpose of this dialogue is to suggest the beginnings of a pastorally sensitive and scripturally based theology of Christian forgiveness.

The present study will not say all that could be said concerning the formulation of a contemporary theology of Christian forgiveness. Its focus is specifically on the insights the Lucan prayer of forgiveness may contribute to a contemporary theology. Therefore, there are numerous theological issues, such as the relationship of the Lucan prayer of forgiveness with ecclesiology, eschatology, sacramental and liturgical life, etc., that will not be systematically addressed in this study. Although the dynamics of the Lucan prayer of forgiveness surely could sustain dialogue with moral theology, especially as this theology understands interpersonal relationships, socio-political issues, and various responses to aggression, this dialogue will not be developed here. Also not elaborated are the contributions the Lucan prayer of forgiveness has to offer the disciplines of spirituality or the sociology of religion. Finally, the contributions of this study toward the furthering of specific therapeutic theories of forgiveness, although potentially rich, will not be outlined within the context of this work.

Although this investigation is limited, its theological import is significant. Various brands of liberationist, feminist, cultural, and political theologies take seriously the problems of evil, violence, and injustice in the contemporary world. To do theology without being aware of this concern would be to do one's pondering in a vacuum. The horrors of modern warfare, the violations of human dignity, and the dehumanizing prejudice of unjust social systems demand that the contemporary Christian theologian reexamine the gospel mandate to forgive.

On the other hand, a theology focused on the problem of evil can easily become bitter, angry, and aggressive. The dialectic tension between naive romanticism and violent zealotry must be maintained in laying the modern theological foundation. When dealing with those who have been oppressed or violated, complicated theological or philosophical systematics are pastorally inappropriate. It is hoped that the reader will find in this study insights obtained from the Lucan prayer of forgiveness that provide understandable and pastorally sensitive foundations for a contemporary understanding of the nature and process of Christian forgiveness.

1

Introducing the Dialogue Partners

Forgiveness: A Pastoral Dilemma

Forgiveness, as witnessed in a great variety of New Testament writings, is essential to Christian holiness. Jesus tells Peter that the offering of forgiveness cannot be calculated. A Christian must forgive not merely seven times but seventy-seven times (Matt 18:21-22). The disciples learn that if they expect their prayer to be efficacious they must forgive those against whom they hold grievances (Mark 11:25). In short, the model of human forgiveness is the forgiveness of God. Christians are called to forgive as unconditionally as God does (Col 3:13).

As these New Testament imperatives are exercised within contemporary life, complex theological and pastoral questions arise. One wonders, for example, how Christians can realistically forgive those who betray the trust foundational to close relationships. Are Christian victims required to forgive significant others who demonstrate contempt toward their well-being? Must children abused by caretakers respond to their perpetrators with unconditional regard? Are spouses, even when their partners show little or no movement toward reformation, required to forgive repeatedly? When faced with betrayals by significant others, how does one imagine, much less effect, Christian forgiveness?

John Patton suggests that because special relationships involve both intense histories and voluntary obligations, one cannot mechanically apply general ethical principles to these relationships. In special relationships one expects that the principles of justice will not only be kept, but will also be transcended in a manner consistent with the degree of personal commitment and fidelity that bonds the relationship.[1]

One could inquire whether the concept of Christian forgiveness is psychologically healthy. Isolation, repression, reversal, undoing, and projection are denial strategies that block the process of true forgiveness. If these strategies are required in a Christian theology of forgiveness, this theology is certainly psychologically suspect. Healthy forgiveness cannot exist when forgiveness "denies that there is anger, acts as if it never happened, smiles as though it never hurt, fakes as though it's all forgotten."[2]

John Gartner speaks of an immature forgiveness, often found in religious circles, that is characterized by a superior smugness. "Often the forgiven one feels insulted rather than reconciled with, understood by, and accepted by the forgiver."[3] A forgiveness based on splitting, the persecutor is bad while I am good, or on projection, I feel hate and therefore the persecutor is hate-filled, cannot be the foundation of a true Christian forgiveness.[4]

If the Christian is required to forgive, especially if this forgiveness is demanded immediately following a violent act or even during it, can the Christian truthfully deal with the volatility of anger generated by victimization? Lewis Smedes will insist that there is anger left over after the act of forgiving another. Because forgiveness does not change the objective facts of the conflict situation, it also does not automatically remove the just anger caused by the violation. Forgiveness, according to Smedes, gradually lessens the malice one feels toward another. What one needs to do with leftover anger is to give it a positive direction. Forgiveness leaves one with an anger which is without malice.[5]

Jeffrey M. Brandsma discusses both the positive and negative effects of anger. Positively, anger defends the self from further or continued abuse, creates needed distance and boundaries, and can provide the energy needed to come to creative and constructive solutions. Negatively, anger can produce destructive fantasies, disproportionate hostility, and free-floating aggression capable of affecting other personal relationships.[6]

After reviewing a number of psychological and religious opinions regarding forgiveness and the problem of anger, Robert D. Enright and Robert L. Zell note that many pastoral counselors recommend that victims be aware of anger and not repress it, but at the same time do not advocate expressing the anger directly to the offender.[7] Richard Fitzgibbons recommends forgiveness therapy as a treatment for anger. He claims that there are three mechanisms available for responding to anger: denial, expression, and forgiveness. He sees forgiveness therapy as more effective than expression therapy in that forgiveness better releases individuals from painful experiences of the past and facilitates the reconciliation of relationships, while expression can often strain already weak relationships.[8]

Dennis and Matthew Linn describe anger as the second stage of forgiveness. If they are healthy, those who are violated experience symptoms of anger. Christian responsibility directs the energy of this anger away from the negative expressions of denial, illness, drinking, etc., and toward positive expressions such as physical labor, exercise, a good cause, etc.[9]

Does the act of Christian forgiveness subject the well-intentioned churchgoer to unhealthy dangers of repressed rage? John Patton suggests that "part of the problem with human forgiveness has been religion's attempt to deal with the rage evoked by injury to the self rather than recognizing that it is the *heart* or self *with the rage in it* that is the problem."[10] The depth of the rage, according to Patton, is an indicator of the depth of the problem and must be pastorally responded to with a proportionate depth of empathy and patience.[11]

Must Christians face the worst with no feeling of hate or hope of revenge? Lewis Smedes disagrees with those who, by arguing that Christians are supposed to "hate the sin and love the sinner,"[12] separate the offender from the deed. Smedes proposes that it is the offender that is truly hated by the victim and not just the deeds of the offender. This is why an offense perpetrated by a close acquaintance often invites the most virulent hate. In discussing the dynamics of forgiveness one is dealing with a complexity of personal relationships and emotions, not merely with a philosophical theory of evil.[13]

Finally, one might wonder if there are circumstances in which retribution rather than forgiveness is justified? Can an attitude of forgiveness include acts of retaliation or confrontation? Although not condoning acts of retaliation, Doris Donnelly affirms the need for confrontation for repeated offenses. This confrontation is an act of Christian love and coexists with the act of forgiveness. "Forgiveness does not abrogate our right, our responsibility, to work peacefully so that injustice does not repeat itself."[14]

Must the forgiver relinquish all forms of compensation? Enright and Zell consider four motives in the Christian struggle to balance justice and forgiveness. Using compensation as a means to seek revenge cannot be Christian. Neither, since this dynamic tends to bind the offender, can demanding compensation in order to balance emotional suffering. If emotional trauma is forgiven and the victim sues only for the necessities of life, the demand for compensation is legitimate. Finally, a Christian could also consider totally releasing the offender from debt.[15]

Does the moral dictum of "doing the truth in love" apply to a violent situation? If so, how does the Christian community struggle to discern truth while at the same time insist that the journey toward truth be grounded and maintained in love? Bernard Häring wrestles with the problem of justice and reconciliation. Objectively speaking, the one who has committed the greater offense is obligated to make the first move toward reconciliation. Under the law of grace, however, the one who has a greater gift of healing and of peace must reach out. One who feels that one cannot forgive because the offender has failed to ask forgiveness needs to ponder this attitude in light of the saving justice of God. "However, sincere love can and must sometimes be reconciled with a moderate and restrained insistence on justice, especially when the rights of third parties and the common good are involved."[16]

R. S. Downie revisits the common assumption that the readiness to forgive is virtuous, while the unwillingness to forgive is a vice. He suggests that this assumption can promote two caricatures of forgiveness: condonation and pardon. In condonation, the victim pretends that the infraction was unoffensive, when the opposite, in fact, is true. To promote such an untruth, especially if this untruth has disproportionate consequences, is morally questionable. By appearing not to forgive, one is actually refusing to condone an evil that has been done. Pardoning involves relinquishing just demands of retribution from an offender. It often is a condonation by one with authority to release an offender from obligation. The difference between pardoning and forgiving, according to Downie, is "that we pardon as officials in social roles but forgive as persons."[17] William R. Neblett speaks of the difficulty of separating the concepts of forgiving and condoning based on performatory utterances. Neblett posits that the concept of forgiveness will never be a pure one. Although a generally forgiving attitude is morally preferable, common sense and experience at times warn against a forgiveness that offers an offender further opportunity to render harm.[18]

The challenge of the contemporary theologian reflecting on forgiveness is to ponder these theological and pastoral questions in light of gospel insights. Although a plentitude of insights could be obtained by critically interpreting each gospel text dealing with forgiveness, the aim of this study is more modest. This work will confine itself to one particular insight from the gospel tradition—the Lucan prayer of forgiveness uttered by Jesus and Stephen during their times of persecution.

The Lucan Prayer of Forgiveness

Even though the labyrinthine dynamics of evil have fascinated artists, playwrights, philosophers, and theologians through the ages, the interdynamics of goodness with their ability to shatter the bondage of evil prove themselves even more complex and intriguing. Myths and stories give rise to ever-broadening reflections on the mystery of good and evil. Paul Ricoeur lists three primitive symbols of evil: stain or defilement, sin before God, and the burden of guilt. These symbols in turn generate narrative or dramatic myths that attempt to articulate the human struggle between good and evil. The leading characters in these myths symbolize the struggle inherent in the human condition. In the Adamic myth, human pain has its origin in the human heart. Salvation or pardon comes through the second Adam who will not only restore the new order, but will also bring about a new creation. Through this second Adam, the human debt is forgiven. Thus, according to Ricoeur, "the symbol of life is saved as a symbol only through communication with the ensemble of the eschatological symbols of justification."[19]

The Christian story, which is certainly one of the most influential and provocative narratives of all times,[20] bases itself on such an intricate plot. The cycles of conflict and evil in the Lucan account are camouflaged by the legitimate facades of government, custom, and religion. This deception makes it difficult to pinpoint an exact source of blame.

René Girard posits that "it is a waste of time to examine, as certain modern commentators do, the unequal way in which the blame in the Gospels is attributed to the various protagonists of the Passion, since to do so indicates an essential misunderstanding of the real purpose of the account."[21] A scapegoat draws crowds like a poor immune system draws a contagious disease. The religious leaders, the political leaders, the common people, and even the disciples play a role in the condemnation of Jesus. The sin of all is the refusal to believe the truth of revelation. Inevitably, this refusal of the truth is externalized as hate-filled persecution of the prophetic person. After the crucifixion, the Paraclete or Advocate speaks on behalf of the victim to vindicate the victim's death. It is this Paraclete who "is truly the spirit of truth that dissipates the fog of mythology."[22]

Because the victim's life bears a truth that brings crisis to the community, the persecutors spill innocent blood in an attempt to restore order and stability. "Apparently, the revelation is a failure; it ends in persecutions that seem likely to smother it but ultimately bring it to fulfillment."[23] The witness of the persecuted one has disturbed the complacency of the communal demons. The evangelical process, by lovingly and insistently

inviting the enemy again into prophetic truth, is completed in
the act of forgiveness. This forgiveness is justified because,
until the persecutors understand the truth being resisted, they
sincerely do not know what they do.[24]

In the reigning confusion leading characters are killed.
These characters, despite an apparent failure in fruitful missions of their own due to the violence, persevere in faith, hope,
and love. The expectations of Jesus as Savior found in the first
chapters of Luke's Gospel are contrasted with the inability of
the crucified Jesus to save himself. The paradox revolves
around the fact that if Jesus would have saved his life, he
would have indeed lost his life (Luke 9:24). In the acceptance
of apparent humiliation and defeat and in placing his total
trust in God, Jesus finds salvation.[25] Thus the Christian tradition and liturgy paradoxically speak of "joy in the cross" and
"victory in death."[26]

Jerome Neyrey develops the theme of the faith of Jesus and
Stephen. The faith of Jesus becomes the salvation of the disciple. However, since the victim is not immediately preserved
from suffering and death, this faith must reside in hope. The
persecutors make the mistake of looking for salvation to occur
immediately (Luke 23:37, 39) but, knowing that God will
vindicate in God's time and in God's way, the victim, suffering
in the spirit of filial confidence, prayerfully endures.[27]

By persevering in the prayer of forgiveness, the persecuted
one demonstrates both love for God and love for the enemy.
Jon Sobrino proposes that "forgiving someone who has hurt
us is an act of love for the offender because we want to relieve
him of his personal failure and not definitely close off his future."[28] It is God who is the foundation of such lavish mercy
(Luke 6:35-36).

The effect is that this faith, hope, and love not only survive
but have evangelical impact. The victory persecution enjoys
against the one who does the will of God appears conclusive
upon the death of the victim but is in fact illusory. Observing
this point, Robert O'Toole proposes that in the Lucan corpus
"persecution fails to achieve its objectives but rather causes
the church to grow, thus constituting a positive element and a
decisive factor in the spread of the word. Paradoxically, perse-

cution itself serves to spread the news of God's saving will."[29] In the Gospel of Luke one of the first fruits of this effectiveness is that Jesus inspires disciples like Stephen who, imitating their master, insist upon praying the prayer of forgiveness even as they shed their blood. Brian Beck suggests that the imitation of Christ especially in the hour of suffering identifies the true disciple. "What Jesus exemplifies in his Passion is the way of loving and forgiveness of enemies to which he has called his followers; as they are to comport themselves under persecution so has he."[30]

This study interprets the prayer of forgiveness of Jesus and Stephen not merely as isolated Scripture passages (Luke 23:34; Acts 7:60) which record the prayer itself, but as relational communication between the persecuted ones, the persecutors, the Church, and the Triune God. The relational context of the prayer focuses on Jesus' and Stephen's perseverance in love of both God and neighbor during their times of passion and on the response of God to their persevering prayer. As one traces this perseverance and its response in the Lucan narrative, one discovers three interrelated dynamics:

(1) *The Prayer of Forgiveness.* Grounded in the unconditional love of God, Jesus prays that God will forgive his persecutors: "Father, forgive them; for they do not know what they are doing" (Luke 23:34). Stephen's prayer is similar: "Lord, do not hold this sin against them" (Acts 7:60).

(2) *The Prayer of Surrender.* Jesus decides to surrender his spirit into the hands of God: "Father, into your hands I commend my spirit" (Luke 23:46). Stephen's prayer is similar but addressed to Jesus: "Lord Jesus, receive my spirit" (Acts 7:59).

(3) *The Action of the Spirit.* God responds efficaciously to the prayers of Jesus and Stephen in the Pentecostal birth of the first Christian community and in the foundation of the Gentile Christian community.[31]

The first dynamic, the petition that God might forgive (Luke 23:34; Acts 7:60), echoes a theme played throughout the Lucan corpus. Zechariah's prophecy introduces the forgiveness theme proclaiming that Jesus will give those who belong to him knowledge of salvation by the forgiveness of their sins (Luke 1:77). For Luke this forgiveness is one way to summarize the effects of the Christ-event. The purpose of Jesus' ministry is to release humans from their debt of guilt before God *(aphesis)*.[32]

Stories unique to Luke develop this theme. The parable of the prodigal son (Luke 15:11-34) contrasts the unconditional forgiveness of the father with the stinginess of the elder brother. This contrast between miserly regard and God's prodigal forgiveness is also illustrated in the parable of the two debtors inserted into the story of the pardon of the sinful woman (Luke 7:36-50).

The ability of the victim to pray the prayer of forgiveness is grounded in God's love. Unconditional love and mercy are Godlike gifts. The capability to love, forgive, bless, and even to excuse the persecutor flows from God's grace. C.F.D. Moule presents Christian forgiveness as a dynamic reality. First of all, forgiveness is a free gift of God. In order to be operative, people need to accept and appropriate this gift. This "gracious free gift of God, in its very acceptance as a free gift, evokes the ultimate output of energy from responsive persons. And in Christ the two sides of this reciprocal movement are already both a reality."[33]

Although the possibility of praying the prayer of forgiveness is rooted in the graciousness of God, the decision to embrace this possibility is made by the victim. To decide to pray the prayer of forgiveness is to open up the possibility of conversion for both oneself and for one's adversary and thus to enable the spirited growth of the Church.

Donald Senior proposes that in his prayer of forgiveness for his enemies "Jesus breathes the same gracious spirit as God. His prayer is in full harmony with God's own lavish and indiscriminate mercy."[34] Eugene LaVerdiere suggests that "now that Jesus was exalted at the Father's right hand (Luke 22:69; Acts 7:56) as Lord, he himself would receive the spirit of those (Acts 7:59) who joined him in forgiving their enemies (Acts 7:60)."[35]

The second dynamic, the prayer of surrender (Luke 23:46; Acts 7:59), portrays Jesus and Stephen, even when all appearances mock their faith, hoping in God's goodness and generativity. During times when the work of interpersonal reconciliation is impeded, Christians persevere in forgiveness by interceding for their persecutors and by surrendering the work of reconciliation into the hands of God. When they are so crippled by violence that they are no longer able to work for justice, Christians who wish to persevere in love must surrender their spirits into the hands of God who alone is able to effect forgiveness (Luke 5:20-21). In the Gospel of Luke this second dynamic, the prayer of surrender, occurs after the petition that God might forgive the persecutors (23:46); in the Acts of the Apostles this order is reversed (7:58-59).

Because the prayer dynamic is relational, the prayer of forgiveness does not end with the decision to petition forgiveness for an oppressor and to surrender one's spirit into the hands of God. Since God plays the grounding and the reciprocal roles in the prayer relationship, one expects a response from God—the third dynamic. In Luke, this expectation is not disappointed. The prayer of forgiveness of both Jesus and Stephen releases the fecund power of the Holy Spirit into the violent domain.

The Lucan prayer of Jesus is immediately effective in the centurion's glorification of God and proclamation of Jesus' innocence (Luke 23:47), and eventually in the Pentecostal creation of the nascent Church (Acts 2). The prayer of Stephen introduces the conversion of Saul and the Gentile mission (Acts 8:4-5).

The creative love of God is invited by the human into the region of chaos and darkness. Overcoming the forces of evil in the world was part of the mission of Isaiah's messianic leader. Luke portrays the activity of the Spirit in the world in conflict with the demonic.[36] The disciples will inherit the Spirit and through their witness will bring the message of salvation to the ends of the earth. Luke presents Jesus appointing the apostles immediately after his enemies, scandalized by his claim to forgive sins, have discussed what their attacks might be against Jesus. Like the mission of Jesus, the disciples' mission will also take them through passion and death.[37]

Schuyler Brown notes the evangelical effect persecution has throughout the Luke-Acts narrative.

And just as God's answer to Jesus' execution was to raise him from the dead, so too does the murder of Jesus' followers have unexpected results. The martyrdom of Stephen leads by scattering the Jerusalem community (Acts 8:1), to the evangelization of Samaria (v. 4f); Paul's journey to martyrdom results in the defense of the gospel before Caesar himself (27:24). The suffering of the martyrs leads to the spread of the Christian kerygma.[38]

It needs to be noted that evangelical effect is not magically appropriated. "What was brought about by Christ in his passion, death, and resurrection and made possible by the gift of the Spirit is appropriated by human beings—in the Lucan view—through faith, repentance and conversion (and baptism)."[39]

In summary, the Lucan prayer of forgiveness is, as is all prayer, grounded in the unconditional love of God. It includes the decisions of Christian victims to pray for their persecutors as well as to surrender their lives to God. Its efficacious nature is demonstrated by the response of God to this prayer which ultimately fulfills the victim's evangelical mission in a generous and creative fashion. After Jesus intercedes for his enemies, "a complicity emerges between this request for forgiveness on the part of the victim and God; it breaks out in the resurrection, for there God makes Jesus' act his own. So we have to read it as a parable of God's action."[40] The prayer is understood as a communication rooted in the creative act of God, responded to through free assent by the victim, and rejoined by God's creative action which uses for its own salvific purpose the evil inflicted against the persecuted one for the creation of Christian community.

Pondering theological and pastoral questions in light of the dynamics of the Lucan prayer of forgiveness is valuable insofar as these Lucan dynamics address the reality of evil without succumbing to a hopelessness that renders blame, righteousness, and resentment more powerful than the Spirit's *koinonia*. Trinitarian life expressed and activated through these prayer dynamics empowers the Christian community by inviting the power of love into the realm of violence, avoids the pitfall of zealotry while maintaining the struggle for justice, and confirms the Christian community in unconditional love grounded in truth.

2

The Context of the
Lucan Prayer of Forgiveness

The Place of Prayer within the Lucan Corpus

Lucan scholars recognize prayer as a theological motif of the Lucan corpus.[1] The Gospel of Luke opens with a narrative portrayal of Luke's theology of prayer. At the hour of incense, when the whole assembly of the people are praying outside, the angel of the Lord appears to Zechariah (Luke 1:8-11). The personal and liturgical prayer of Zechariah united with the communal prayer of the people invites the power of God to enter. God answers this prayer not only by giving Zechariah a son, but also by giving the community a prophet who will announce the coming of the Messiah.

God responds to prayer in Luke in ways that are generous, creative, and often surprising. Prayer is linked to the birth of John the Baptist (1:13), the descent of the Holy Spirit at the baptism of Jesus (3:21), the call of the twelve apostles (6:12-16), and the graced acknowledgment by Peter of Jesus' Messiahship (9:18-20).[2]

Throughout the Gospel, Jesus perseveres in prayer (Luke 3:21; 9:18; 9:29; 22:32). The passion account is outlined with the prayer of Jesus (22:40-42; 23:34, 46). The Gospel concludes with the eleven apostles continually praising God in the Temple (24:53).

In the Acts of the Apostles the Church is born within the context of persevering prayer. While waiting for the promised gift of the Holy Spirit, the women and disciples devote themselves to prayer (1:14). Before selecting Judas's successor, the early community prays (1:24-25). The new believers in the Church devote themselves to the breaking of the bread and to the prayers (2:42). The nascent Church prays with Peter and John after the chief priests and elders attempt to silence them. As the Church prays for the gift of boldness in speaking the Word of God, the place shakes and they speak with the boldness for which they had begged (4:23-31). When Samaritan converts appear, the disciples pray over them and consequently the Samaritans are filled with the Holy Spirit. This outpouring of the Holy Spirit manifests to the early community God's will that Gentiles be welcomed (8:14-17). Likewise, throughout the entire missionary activity of Paul, prayer is central (16:16, 25; 20:36; 21:5; 27:35; 28:8).[3]

Even from such a cursory review, it is evident that the Lucan corpus is set within the milieu of individual and corporate prayer.[4] Since the theme of prayer can be found during every major event of the life of Jesus and of the early Church, the reader discovers that the true disciple is one who must persevere in prayer (Luke 11:5-8; 18:1). Luke portrays the early Church as performing this duty in common. Before Pentecost the apostles, Mary, and some women and other disciples pray together in the upper room (Acts 1:14). In order to free the apostles for prayer and for preaching, Stephen and the other assistants are appointed to serve at tables (6:3-5). The early community prays for the deliverance of Peter (Acts 12:5); they lay hands upon Saul and Barnabas in prayer as they depart on mission (Acts 13:3).[5]

The frequency of prayer terms in the Lucan corpus could point to Luke's theological development of the prayer theme. In contrast to nineteen instances in Luke[6] and sixteen in Acts,[7] the verb *proseuchomai,* which means to pray or to petition, occurs eleven times in Mark[8] and sixteen in Matthew.[9] Its cognate noun *proseuchē,* while occurring three times in Luke[10] and nine times in Acts,[11] is found three times in Matthew[12] and twice in Mark.[13] This means that, while Matthew uses *proseuchomai* and its cognate nineteen times, Mark thirteen times, and John not at all, the Lucan corpus uses this prayer term and its cognate forty-seven times.[14] In addition, Luke also includes prayer texts that do not use a specific prayer term. The prayer of forgiveness and the prayer of surrender uttered from the cross (Luke 23:34, 46) are such examples.[15]

These statistics can, however, be misleading. When one considers the relative extensiveness of the Lucan corpus in contrast to the other New Testament books, the difference in the frequency of prayer terms used does not seem as disproportionate. To establish the importance of the theme of prayer in Luke it is more useful to argue the pivotal placement of the prayer terms or, in the absence of specific prayer terms, the placement of actual prayers rather than the frequency of these prayers or prayer terms.[16]

Oscar Gerald Harris notes that when contrasting Luke's use of prayer terms with Mark and Q, Luke is found to have sixteen prayer terms in places where his sources do not and that these terms appear at significant moments in the gospel.[17] When comparing the contribution of Luke to the rest of the New Testament, Luke's emphasis on prayer[18] and his vocabulary for prayer are extensive.[19]

It is of prime importance to Luke that a Christian or the Christian community pray during times of crisis and decision making:

> Prayer is mentioned by Luke at important points in his account of Jesus and the early church. Jesus' baptism, transfiguration, agony and crucifixion are turning points in Luke's narrative. Likewise, the church in Jerusalem waiting for the gift of the Spirit and choosing Judas' replacement, facing persecution, the Samaritan mission, the conversion of Cornelius, and Paul's first journey which eventuates in the Gentile mission are important for Luke's entire presentation.[20]

Prayer is related to significant events in Jesus' life and ministry,[21] and therefore, also to the course of salvation history.[22] Prayer opens the Christian to the will of God and to the power of God. The power of prayer in Luke inaugurates the day of salvation promised to Israel. This day of salvation is to be a time when prayer is fulfilled.[23] It will be a day when people of all nations join together in universal praise of God (Isa 56:6-7; Mal 1:11).

The frequent mention of the fulfillment of prayer in the opening chapters of Luke's Gospel signals the arrival of the day of salvation (Luke 1:55, 68-69; 2:11, 30-32). It is the child Jesus who is the advent figure of this new age.

This theme of the fulfillment of prayer is intricately tied not only to Jesus' birth but also to his life and his mission. Jesus is presented by Luke as one who habitually prays. In referring to the prayer of Jesus, Luke expresses iterative action suggesting that Jesus was in the habit of praying (5:16).[24] Petitionary prayer in the Lucan corpus is an avenue through which the disciple seeks the will of God. One discovers the Father's will by searching for this will in prayer.[25] The intention of Jesus' prayer is not primarily to give himself relief from the pressures of the needy crowds, but rather to allow the Father to guide him along the purposes of salvation history.

One of the disciples, observing Jesus at prayer, asks Jesus to teach his followers to pray just as John taught his disciples (Luke 11:1). In response to this request, Jesus teaches his disciples the Lord's Prayer. Such a petition does not suggest that this disciple lacked the basic Jewish formation in prayer and liturgical discipline. Rather, it was common for Jewish groups to distinguish themselves by common prayer forms.[26] The disciple asked Jesus for a prayer that might distinguish the company of Jesus from that of other religious groups. The disciples of John the Baptist had such distinguishing prayer forms as did the Pharisees and the Qumran community.[27]

The nascent Church found in the Lord's Prayer the fundamental dynamics of Jesus' life and teaching. The disciple who wishes to follow Jesus must learn to imitate him in prayer. The disciples, like Jesus, pray in order that they might not be subjected to the test (Luke 22:46). Without this ceaseless prayer, the followers of Jesus make themselves vulnerable to the temptation of apostasy. Ceaseless communion with God becomes the mark of Christian faith.[28]

There are instances where Matthew and Mark record Jesus praying while Luke does not. After the healings at Capernaum, while Luke 4:42 mentions Jesus leaving the crowds for a deserted place, Mark 1:35 portrays Jesus at prayer. Matthew 14:23 and Mark 6:46 describe Jesus praying after the feeding of the five thousand, while Luke does not mention this prayer. Yet, it must be noted that Luke has seven unique portraits of the praying Jesus. Luke mentions that Jesus prayed before his baptism (3:21); before his first collision with the scribes and Pharisees over his right to forgive sins (5:16); before calling his disciples (6:12);[29] before the first prediction of the passion event (9:18); at the Transfiguration (9:29); before the disciples asked for the Lord's Prayer (11:1); and when dying on the cross (23:34, 46).[30]

In addition, the Gospel of Luke contains three unique prayer parables. In the first the disciple is admonished to be as persistent in prayer as the inopportune friend (11:5-13). In the second Luke examines this same theme of persistence through the story of the poor widow and the unjust judge (18:1-8).[31] Although Allison Trites sees the central focus of the parable of the Pharisee and the publican (18:9-14) as righteousness and not prayer, this parable does offer insight into the relationships between prayer, attitudes, and efficacy.[32]

Luke records Jesus' prayer for Peter that his faith may not fail (22:31-32), and while Matthew 26:36 and Mark 14:32 describe Jesus as telling his disciples to "sit here, while I pray," and later on in the narrative Peter, James, and John are asked to "keep awake and pray," Luke alone portrays Jesus as exhorting his apostles to pray that they "may not come into the time of trial" (22:40).

In summary, one can observe that prayer is a theme central to Luke. Its numerous occurrences as well as the pivotal placements of the prayer motif within the Lucan corpus signal its theological importance. Perseverance in prayer becomes a distinguishing mark of the faithful disciple and of the early Church.

Manuscript Evidence and the Prayer for Persecutors

It should be noted that a number of the early and important manuscripts of the Gospel of Luke omit Jesus' prayer for his persecutors (Luke 23:34).[33] Although no attempt will be made here to validate the petition for the forgiveness of the persecutors as part of the original gospel, its inclusion in the gospel, even if this was the work of an editor, and its survival throughout the Christian tradition attest to its relevance. Alexander B. Bruce remarks that the prayer of Jesus in Luke 23:34 is "a prayer altogether true to the spirit of Jesus, therefore, though reported by Lk. alone, intrinsically credible. It is with sincere regret that one is compelled, by its omission in important MSS., to regard its genuineness as subject to a certain amount of doubt."[34] Paul Scherer, in his exposition on Luke's twenty-third chapter, while recognizing the manuscript difficulties, refers to the prayer of forgiveness as "one of the most typically 'Christian' utterances credited to Jesus in the Gospel tradition."[35]

Bruce M. Metzger argues against those who claim that the verse's omission from primary manuscripts was a deliberate excision by copyists who, prompted by the fall of Jerusalem, believed that Jesus' prayer of forgiveness for the Jews had gone unheeded and could not tolerate such evidence. Although admitting the textual difficulties, Metzger proposes that "the logion, though probably not part of the original Gospel of Luke, bears self-evident tokens of its dominical origin, and was retained, within double square brackets, in its traditional place where it had been incorporated by unknown copyists relatively early in the transmission of the Third Gospel."[36]

Most modern scholars, while respecting the manuscript evidence, view the passage as authentic Lucan theology. I. Howard Marshall concludes that "the balance of the evidence thus favours acceptance of the saying as Lucan, although the weight of the textual evidence against the saying precludes any assurance in opting for this verdict."[37] In describing the manuscript evidence for including the prayer and for excluding the prayer as "very evenly balanced," G.W.H. Lampe expresses this same viewpoint.[38]

Robert J. Karris presents an argument based on internal evidence supporting the passage's authenticity. Both the language and the thought of the prayer are Lucan. The prayer of Stephen seems to purposely parallel the prayer of Jesus. The crucifixion narrative contains sayings of Jesus in each major section, and the prayer conforms with Luke's theology of Jesus as the rejected prophet who practices and preaches the forgiveness of sins. Because of this type of evidence, Karris, unlike Metzger, sides with those who speculate that the verse was excised by copyists who, after the destruction of Jerusalem, felt that the prayer of Jesus was ineffective for the Jews.[39]

Because of its inclusion in early and significant manuscripts, the textual authenticity of Stephen's prayer for forgiveness (Acts 7:60) is undisputed.[40] Some scholars suggest that the prayer of Stephen may have influenced the inclusion of the prayer of forgiveness on the lips of Jesus in the Gospel text.[41]

If the petition for the persecutors was an addition to the original gospel, evidence suggests that this addition would have been an early one. Some early Church Fathers refer to this petition from the Gospel of Luke in their writings. In the "Epistula ad Ephesios," Ignatius of Antioch invokes the reader to imitate the Lord who when threatened did not counter with threats but instead prayed, "Father, forgive them; they know not what they do" (Luke 10:10-12). Irenaeus in *Adversus Haereses III* continues this same theme referring to the prayer in 16:9 and 18:5. The historian Eusebius, relying upon Hegesippus who Eusebius claims lived immediately after the apostles, recounts the death of James the brother of the Lord. According to Eusebius, Hegesippus's fifth book of his memoirs pictures James, a leader in the Jerusalem church, as one who was constantly on his knees in the Temple, begging forgiveness for the people. Eusebius, in portraying the murder of James, has the scribes and Pharisees quoting Isaiah 3:10 as they rush in rage to stone James. James, when dying, echoes the Lord in the prayer of forgiveness (Luke 23:3-17).

In conclusion, one can observe that although the Lucan petition for forgiveness of the persecutors is indeed missing from important early manuscripts of the Gospel of Luke, scholars argue that its language and theology are Lucan. There are those who lean toward its authenticity on the basis of internal evidence. Certainly its relevance to Christian faith is confirmed through its use in early Christian literature. Whether the Lucan text was inserted or excised for a time is not essential to this discussion. What is essential is that the Lucan prayer of forgiveness is considered by both scholars and tradition to be a prayer faithful to the theology of Luke and to the message of Jesus.

The Fidelity of God as Foundational
to the Prayer of Forgiveness

Foundational to the Lucan prayer of forgiveness is Jesus' and Stephen's personal experiential knowledge of the faithful love of God. Karris has gone so far as to claim that the cardinal point of Lucan theology is that it is a "theology of the faithful God."[42] Although the time for the realization of promises often requires waiting, the God of Luke is a God who is faithful (Luke 1:20; 2:29-31; 24:44; Acts 13:32-33). The God who promised and brought salvation to the Jewish people now continues this saving work.[43]

The disciple is assured that all that happens is the result of this faithful purpose and initiative of God (Acts 4:28). Luke stresses the supremacy of God over all that occurs within the world. The Lucan world unfolds according to the plan of God. It was God who brought Israel out of slavery and established the kingdom of Israel (Acts 13:16-22). It was God who designed the master plan of salvation that would be fulfilled in Jesus (Luke 24:44-47). It was God who ordained that the Good News be proclaimed first to the Jews and then to the Gentiles (Acts 13:46-47).[44]

The life of Jesus unfolds in accordance with this design. This is illustrated in Jesus' life through his birth announced by the divine messenger (Luke 1:26-38), in the opening of his ministry in Nazareth (Luke 4:17-21), and eventually in his passion and resurrection (Luke 24:26-32). Jesus' life develops as it was written by the prophets (Luke 18:31; 22:37; Acts 3:18). The life of John the Baptist unfolds in the same way (Luke 3:4; 7:27).[45]

Similarly, the nascent Church develops according to the plan of God. The promised Spirit breaks forth, "when the day of Pentecost had come" (Acts 2:1). The faithful God chooses witnesses to preach the Good News (Acts 10:41; 22:14-16;

26:16), and like Jesus, what occurs in the life of these witnesses is an unfolding of the divine plan of God (Acts 9:1-19; 27:24).[46]

Because God is sovereign many things "must" be: Jesus "must" be in his Father's house (Luke 2:49);[47] since it is for this purpose that he had been sent, he "must" preach the Kingdom to other towns (Luke 4:43); the Father "must" celebrate his wayward son's return (Luke 15:32); Jesus "must" stay at Zacchaeus' house (Luke 19:5); and finally Jesus "must" suffer and die (Luke 9:22; 17:25; 22:37; 24:7, 44; Acts 17:3).[48] It is divine necessity which is at the root of election. One is chosen by God for a mission. Divine sovereignty is inherent to this mission and propels it toward fulfillment.[49]

One becomes a disciple by discovering through prayer, through the faithful imitation and following of Jesus, and through one's life in community who one is created to be. This experiential knowledge of the sovereign plan of God central to one's personal divine election enables one to become a disciple in imitation of Christ and places one under divine obligation.[50] The root of all discipleship is located within the experience of a personal vocational summons. One becomes a disciple by accepting, as Jesus did, one's unique call which contains the seed of one's destiny (Luke 1:26-35; 2:31-38; 3:21-22).[51]

Martin Dibelius claims that Jesus died as an innocent martyr. This position is disputed by Frank Matera who insists that Jesus was more than a martyr. "The martyr endures unjust persecution and suffering as a righteous sufferer, but Jesus undergoes the passion because it is his *destiny* as Messiah to suffer."[52]

Robert J. Karris also disagrees with the Dibelius position. Although there are parallels such as the struggle against the power of evil, the theme of innocence, the mocking of the victim by the bystanders, the willingness and composure of the martyr's death, and the example of the martyr to the rest of the faith community, Karris argues that the parallels drawn between martyrdom literature and the passion of Jesus are often vague. Karris criticizes those who conclude that Jesus died as an innocent martyr because; (1) there are features of martyrdom literature missing from the passion of Jesus such as the martyr's condemnation of his murderers and the description of the physical agony of the martyr; (2) the parallels of fighting against the power of evil can be given more plausible interpretations; and (3) positions claiming Jesus as an innocent martyr fail to understand the literary and theological importance of the passion narrative within the context of the entire Gospel.[53]

Becoming a faithful disciple in response to one's created identity/vocation (Luke 3:21-22) evokes anger and rejection by some who are unable to manipulate this personal sense of authority (Luke 4:16-30; 12:49-53; 20:1-8; Acts 7:54).[54] This anger and rejection can eventually erupt in persecution (Luke 12:1-12; Acts 8:1-3; 11:19).

Jesus' ability to expose secret attitudes contrary to the purpose of God (Luke 5:21-22; 6:8; 9:46-47; 24:38) escalates the tension. Simeon's prophecy (Luke 2:34-35) announces this interior resistance as the root of Christian persecution. God's salvation will come into direct conflict with the dark inconsistencies of the human heart.[55]

Yet, even as it kills the faithful disciple, evil does not have the last word. The irony of salvation is that God's will can be fulfilled in the midst of evil thus shattering evil's reign (Acts 2:23-24). Jerome Kodell claims that "the great irony here lies in the fact that by causing Jesus' death, Satan is fulfilling the Father's will and causing his own reign of sin to be shattered. The death of Jesus is a crime of men, but it is also, and more importantly, an achievement of God" (Acts 2:23).[56]

One's faith in the fidelity of God is supremely tested during moments of violence. Although persecution is alluded to within the historical context of the Lucan community, scholars debate the exact form of this persecution. There is a strong position which proposes that the Lucan church was indeed a church which was harassed by both Jews and Romans. This persecution, however, was for the most part unofficial and irregular.[57] Luke indicates that some kind of persecution did take place after the martyrdom of Stephen (Acts 8:1-3),[58] and he attributes blame to the religious leaders for the crucifixion of Jesus (Luke 22:1-2; 23:10) and the martyrdom of Stephen (Acts 6:8-14).

Pinpointing the blameworthy proponents of Jesus' crucifixion has evoked much educated discussion.[59] Historians claim that Jerusalem in the first century was a hotbed of radicals and revolutionaries.[60] Where Jesus fit into this political agenda is elusive. It is difficult to assign him a particular bias.[61] Even the religious leaders who seem to be portrayed by Luke as the most blameworthy characters are not totally segregated from Jesus' promised Kingdom. After the crucifixion it is a member of the council, Joseph of Arimathea, who takes it upon himself to bury Jesus (Luke 23:50-56). It is a Pharisee in the Sanhedrin, Gamaliel, who presents the argument responsible for preserving the life of Peter (Acts 5:33-40).

Tannehill illustrates Luke's ability to avoid simplistic categorizations of blame. Important exceptions such as Jairus (Luke 8:41), those Pharisees concerned for Jesus' safety (Luke 13:31), Joseph of Arimathea (Luke 23:50-53), and Gamaliel (Acts 5:33-40) prevent such generalizations. Lucan discipleship is a matter of conversion of heart rather than a matter of party loyalty.[62]

Although one must admit that the Lucan corpus does tend to place most of the blame for the deaths of both Jesus and Stephen on the Jewish religious leaders,[63] this attribution of blame is not the climax of the story. Rather than becoming stuck in the mire of resentment and finger-pointing, however justified this may be, the victims of Luke's account radiate peace, forgiveness, and light. Jesus appears after the resurrection bringing peace, joy, and enlightenment (Luke 24:13-49). Stephen is said to have a face "like the face of an angel" (Acts 6:15).

W.H.C. Frend speaks of Stephen's angelic countenance as having eschatological significance. Stephen's countenance proves that he was already enjoying the bliss reserved for those who have survived the judgment. "He not only had a vision of the world beyond, but provided proof of the outpouring of the Spirit which traditionally was to be the sign of the end of the existing age."[64] The Lucan message is not that the Christian must suffer, but rather that through the inevitable suffering, the Holy Spirit perseveres, and ironically is even better able to fulfill the plan of God.

Besides the possibility of eschatological vision for the victim, martyrdom in the Lucan literature has evangelical effects. The death of Jesus leads to the conversion of the good thief

(Luke 23:39-43) and to the profession of belief in Jesus' innocence by the centurion (Luke 23:47). The death of Stephen
results in the spread of the gospel (Acts 11:19-26). This understanding of the purpose and the efficacious nature of suffering
for one's faith in Jesus is the foundation of Christian peace and
joy.[65]

Faith and trust in the unconditional love of God, even amid
suffering and persecution, is a prerequisite of genuine Christian discipleship (Luke 7:36-50; 12:22-34).[66] This faith and trust,
exercised and tested throughout the disciple's journey, allows
the follower of Christ to believe and to hope in the power of
God even in the moment of desolation and violence. "Salvation is to be found not in fleeing death nor in using one's
power to escape from it, but in trusting that God is righteous
and remains united with his rejected and battered creation
even in its sorest hours."[67]

For Jesus, the fruits of the faith-filled journey culminate in
the journey to Jerusalem. Fitzmyer explains that to be a Lucan
follower of Christ "one has to follow him along the road that
he walks to his destiny in Jerusalem, his *exodus*, his transit to
the Father."[68] This journey to Jerusalem eventually becomes
the corporate journey of the early Church and is referred to as
"the Way" (Acts 9:2; 19:9, 23; 22:4; 24:14, 22). In death, Jesus
and Stephen breathe forth their spirits in total trust and surrender. In the end it is this faith that opens humankind to the
saving power of God, and it is this salvation that eventually
brings the victim's vocation to its true fruition.[69]

In summary, one can see that true disciples are grounded in
God's love for them and, in spite of the harsh reality of violence, continue to believe and to hope in the fidelity of God.
For Luke, all of history is salvation history; thus all historical
and present events must be understood with the eyes of faith.

This divine fidelity functions as both a gift and a task. Insofar as God guarantees the fulfillment of the divine plan, it is a
gift. No matter what the tactic of evil, this tactic is no match for
the infinitely creative action of God. Even if God must inau-
gurate a surprise reversal, God's will is carried out.

Divine fidelity is also a task for the disciple. The follower of
Jesus listens in order to obey and execute the divine plan of

God. The disciples are called to creative action in doing their part in the fulfillment of the divine task, but when this fails, they are to commend their spirits into the hands of God who will confirm, validate and ultimately accomplish their mission.

The Prayer of Forgiveness within the Passion Narratives of Jesus and Stephen

Grounded in the unconditional love of God, the Lucan victim, even in the midst of excruciating torment, is given the grace to persevere in faith-filled and hope-filled prayer. The theme of perseverance in prayer is predominant in Luke's Gospel. Both the parable of the friend at midnight (Luke 11:5-8) and the unjust judge and the persistent widow (Luke 18:1-8) demonstrate the need for such perseverance in prayer.[70] Although Jesus begs his disciples to pray that they might be saved from the test, it becomes obvious that Jesus must undergo the test.[71] It is his life of obedience to the will of the Father which leads him to the moment of crucifixion.[72]

The devil, who had been told not to put the Lord to the test (Luke 4:12), returns after departing for a time (Luke 4:13). Having finished every temptation (Luke 4:13), the power of darkness descends in full force (Luke 22:53).[73] While Jesus preached in the temple area during the daylight, Judas, whom Satan had entered (Luke 22:3), betrays during the night. In the end, this power of darkness seems to conquer not only the fickle hearts of humanity, but also the light of the sun itself (Luke 23:44).[74]

Unlike their master, the disciples trust in the power of the sword rather than in strength of persevering prayer. Hans Conzelmann sees the passage concerning Jesus' command to buy a sword (Luke 22:36) as central to the Gospel of Luke. While Jesus was with them, the disciples participated in the foretaste of future salvation. With the passion, however, a new period is inaugurated. "When Jesus was alive, was the time of salvation; Satan was far away, it was a time without temptation (cf. Luke iv, 13 with xxii, 3 and xxii, 35). Since the Passion, however, Satan is present again and the disciples of Jesus are again subject to temptation (xxii, 36)."[75]

Brown critiques Conzelmann's exegesis. He suggests that the diabolical departure did not suspend all diabolical activity. Rather he proposes that "the devil kept out of Jesus' way. The battle continues, but the devil has been thrown on the defensive; he avoids as far as he can a further encounter with Jesus."[76]

Paul Minear understands that Jesus' betrayal, according to the Lucan account, is threefold. Judas betrays as Jesus had prophesized (Luke 22:21-22). Secondly, the apostles demonstrate their disobedience, in stark contrast to their master, by their possession of swords (Luke 22:38; 49-50). The fact that they possessed two swords "provides the *double* witness required by Deuteronomy and insisted upon by Luke, a witness to the fulfillment of Isa. liii 12."[77] Jesus' healing of the ear attests to his opposition to the use of the sword in his defense (Luke 22:51). Thirdly, the possession of swords also identifies the soldiers as belonging to the hour of darkness (Luke 22:52-53).[78]

Ford perceives the image of the swords as "central to Luke's theology of the passion and to the understanding of Jesus' teaching on nonviolence and nonresistance."[79] For the true disciple of Jesus, there is no need for the sword. Those who bear swords associate themselves with the power of darkness. Neyrey points out that Luke 22:49, unlike Mark, demonstrates that all the disciples were willing to draw the sword. Jesus' response to this situation is curt and to the point (Luke 22:51). His action of healing the ear follows his word of reprimand. Once they possess the Spirit of Jesus, the disciples in the Acts of the Apostles endure trials, death, imprisonment, persecutions, etc., but they do not resort to using the sword. In the Gospel "it is the apostles who are 'the lawless' with whom Jesus is reckoned; they misunderstand Jesus' final words and produce actual swords when Jesus had forecast future difficulties."[80]

Matera finds the sword motif a foil to illustrate the trust of Jesus in the salvific action of the Father. While the disciples trust in their swords "Jesus, by contrast, refuses such protection. He finds his strength in prayer to the Father."[81] Upon arriving at his destination, Jerusalem, Jesus cleanses the Temple (Luke 19:45-46). Although the people continue to hang on to his every word (Luke 19:48), the chief priests and scribes seek to put him to death (Luke 19:47). These religious leaders, because they feared the people (Luke 20:19), find it difficult to execute their desire. Meanwhile, the people are getting up early each morning to listen to Jesus speak in the Temple area (Luke 21:38). Among the common people, the authority of Jesus has replaced that of the chief priests and the scribes. Because Jesus has deprived them of their authority within the Temple area, the chief priests and scribes plot to kill him.[82]

In the midst of the frustrated confusion of the religious leaders desiring the death of Jesus but yet not willing to bear the repercussions of an angry crowd, Judas and Satan enter. What happens in the crucifixion is more than mere human tragedy. What is at stake here is the root eschatological struggle. Yet, even in the midst of such chaos, the human characters are not rendered devoid of responsibility. It is clear that Judas is guilty of accepting a bribe (Luke 22:5), and that the other disciples are negligent in both strength of character and in prayer during the decisive hour (Luke 22:46).[83]

Although the conduct of Jesus during the Lucan passion narrative is an example for Christian discipleship, the trial of Jesus transcends Christian tribulations. There is a messianic character to Jesus' temptation. One does not witness in the passion of Jesus a mere testing of faith, but rather an attempt on Satan's part to frustrate the divine plan of salvation. Although the hardships of Christians are a continuation of the passion of Christ, the fullness of the messianic trial of Jesus is not continued within the Christian life.[84]

Jesus approaches the situation of violence with his eyes wide open. He clearly reads the signs of the times and warns the disciples of the trial awaiting them (Luke 9:22, 44-45; 19:31-33). He proceeds resolutely towards Jerusalem, not as an anxious martyr but rather as a person resolved to be faithful to his God-given mission.[85]

Luke differs from the other Synoptics in that he places the agony of Jesus on the Mount of Olives and does not mention the garden of Gethsemane (22:39). Moreover, Jesus is accompanied not only by Peter, James, and John, but by all the disciples (Luke 22:39). Only once, unlike Matthew and Mark's three times (Matt 26:36-45; Mark 14:35-41), does Jesus pray for deliverance (Luke 22:42). Thus, unlike the accounts of Matthew and Mark, there is no need for Jesus to rouse himself between his petitions in order to wake the sleeping disciples.

Instead of stressing the agonizing abandonment of Jesus, Luke also differs from Matthew and Mark in that he focuses attention on the determination of Jesus to do the will of the Father.[86] One who wishes to do the will of the Father must listen in prayer. Luke uses the scene on the Mount of Olives as a lesson in perseverance in prayer. While the disciples depict what happens to those who do not persevere in prayer, Jesus is the model of persevering prayer in the face of temptation. The bracketing of the passage with the instruction of Jesus to his disciples that they pray so that they might be spared the test (Luke 22:40, 46) further illustrates Luke's intention to demonstrate the necessity of perseverance in prayer.[87]

The fruits of this perseverance are illustrated throughout the Lucan passion narrative. Jesus, who has accepted the will of the Father and acts in accordance with the salvific plan, has authority over the chaos of evil. When Judas goes forth to kiss Jesus, Jesus challenges him with a question (Luke 22:48). Unlike Mark 14:45, it is quite uncertain in Luke's rendition whether Judas actually kissed or even touched Jesus. When the sword is used, Jesus immediately heals (Luke 22:51). When the sinner repents, Jesus extends forgiveness and the promise of paradise (Luke 23:43). Even in the moment of violence Jesus heals and forgives. "Such behavior on the part of Jesus results from his faithfulness to prayer and his acceptance of the Father's will."[88]

The fruits of prayerful perseverance can be illustrated by comparing Jesus, the one who persevered in prayer, with Peter, the one who slept. While Jesus, maintaining his dignity and authority, allows himself to be arrested, Peter, because of fear, denies his affiliation with Jesus. Since he has failed to persevere in prayer, Peter denies. Because Peter's denial in the Lucan account takes place in the presence of Jesus, it is even more poignant. Luke, unlike Matthew and Mark, states that after Peter's denial the Lord turned around and looked at Peter (Luke 22:61).[89]

Jesus promises that his followers will be persecuted, but also guarantees that at the moment of persecution he will give them the words and the wisdom to respond to their adversaries (Luke 21:13-15).[90] This is demonstrated in the life of Stephen (Acts 6:10). Stephen, like Jesus, is able to see the interior hardness of heart of the Jewish religious leaders. Stephen's speech against them challenges inner attitudes which have resisted the Spirit of God (Acts 7:51-52).[91]

Like Jesus, Stephen suffers and is vindicated by God.[92] Discipleship requires that followers understand that they too may be required to suffer and die for the sake of the gospel. Yet death does not have the final word. It is through death that the disciple's mission to reveal the light to the nations and the glory of Israel (Luke 2:31-32) is fulfilled.[93] On the day of Stephen's martyrdom a persecution began which scattered the church of Jerusalem. This scattering was the impetus of the Gentile mission (Acts 8:1, 4).

Stephen speaks the truth with passion and as a result of his incendiary speech is stoned. Like Jesus who also spoke harsh words of truth to those with hardened hearts, Stephen does not retaliate during the moment of violence. Instead, Stephen prays for his persecutors and begs forgiveness for their evil deed. Although the Church suffers violence throughout the Acts of the Apostles, there is not one instance of the Church responding violently to persecution.[94]

Luke carefully parallels the death of Stephen with the death of Jesus.[95] In Acts 7:56, Stephen has a vision of the Son of Man standing at the throne of God. This fulfills Jesus' prophesy uttered before the Sanhedrin that the Son of Man would be seated at the right hand of the power of God (Luke 22:69). Jesus prays for forgiveness for his persecutors (Luke 23:34), as does Stephen (Acts 7:60). As Jesus entrusts his spirit into the hands of the Father with a loud voice (Luke 23:46), so does Stephen, also with a loud voice, hand his spirit over to the Lord Jesus (Acts 7:59). Like Jesus whose prayer of forgiveness bears fruit in the repentance of the crucified thief,[96] Stephen, through his prayer of forgiveness for the persecutors, opens up possibilities for conversion. That repentance and conversion are possible even for those who actively persecute the witnesses of the risen Lord is evident in the conversion of Saul. God's creative possibilities cannot be conquered by the violence of evil.

To conclude, one observes in both Lucan volumes the prayer of forgiveness spoken during times of agony and violence. On the cross Jesus fulfills his own command to persist in prayer (Luke 22:39-42, 45-46). Prayer becomes the support which enables the disciple to persevere through persecution (Luke 18:7-8; 21:36). Because Jesus is obedient to his own words, his prayer that he might not fail the test is granted. Jesus perseveres in faith, hope and love for both God and for his persecutors. The model disciple Stephen endures in a like manner.[97]

Having explored the role of prayer in the Lucan corpus, the manuscript evidence for the petition that God might forgive the persecutor (Luke 23:34; Acts 7:60), the importance of God's fidelity in the work of Luke, and the prayer of forgiveness within the passion narratives of Jesus and Stephen, one must proceed to probe more deeply the process of the Lucan prayer of forgiveness. Three dynamics of this process have already been outlined in Chapter 1: namely, Christian victims must first will to petition for the forgiveness of their persecutors; victims must surrender their spirits over in trust into the hands of God; and finally, God responds to the prayers of Christian victims. The exploration of these dynamics is the task of the next chapter.

3

The Process of the
Lucan Prayer of Forgiveness

The First Dynamic

"Father, forgive them; for they do not know what they are doing"
(Luke 23:34)

"Lord, do not hold this sin against them" (Acts 7:60)

The first dynamic of the prayer of forgiveness requires a number of interrelated considerations. First, the prayer of forgiveness is a decision. Jesus and Stephen choose to pray for those who persecute them. Second, this decision to forgive is not executed by the victims themselves but is rather a petition that another might forgive the persecutors. Third, the theme of forgiveness within the Lucan corpus needs further exploration in order to understand what the persecuted one is praying for. Finally, one wonders for whom Jesus and Stephen are praying. In the gospel account the "they," who are the object of the prayer, are not only forgiven but are even excused on the grounds of ignorance and lack of understanding.

The Prayer of Forgiveness as a Decision

Jesus teaches his disciples that the decision to forgive those in their debt grounds the prayer of those desiring to be true followers (Luke 11:4). The forgiveness of one's neighbor is to be extended with prodigal generosity (Luke 17:3-4). Communion with God is possible only through the decision to forgive one's neighbor. Christian community happens when those who are already members actively decide to forgive those who have persecuted them.[1]

Similar to the prayer on the Mount of Olives (Luke 22:42), the prayer asking forgiveness brings together in word and act a central theme of the Lucan corpus.[2] The Good News of forgiveness, which Jesus so insistently proclaims throughout the Gospel and which the early Church proclaims with great fervor,[3] is chosen even in situations of violence. While violence reduces persons to objects, the decision to pray for forgiveness invites persons back into personhood and hopes for reconciliation.

When one's hands are prevented from doing good to the neighbor because of violence, one can decide to continue to love the oppressor through prayer (Luke 6:27-28). It is the power of God that is the saving, forgiving power. Forgiveness is not merely a reward for adequate repentance and prayerfulness but is, rather, a free and unconditional gift of God. One decides to pray for the forgiveness of the neighbor because one is motivated by God's own lavish mercy (Luke 6:35-36; 15:11-32). Like Jesus and Stephen, the Christian is called upon to forgive even before the persecutor offers a sign of repentance.[4]

A retaliatory prayer attitude which begs for the protection of Israel and for the defeat and the humiliation of her enemies (e.g., Pss 6:8-10; 140:6-13; 2 Maccabees 7) is challenged by the prayer of forgiveness.[5] The decision to pray for one's oppressor is effective not because it necessarily reverses violence, but because it opens the one praying to the divine will of God. This will of God has authority over the power of evil and, in order that the Church might continue to witness to the power of salvation, creatively breaks through the bondage of darkness.

The response of Stephen to those stoning him differs greatly from the Old Testament figure Zechariah, son of Jehoiada, who suffered the same fate. As Zechariah is about to breathe his last, he prays that God might see his plight and avenge his enemies (2 Chr 24:22). Although the deaths by stoning are similar, the responses to death are very different. Stephen does not model his response on that of Zechariah. Rather, Stephen proves himself to be a true disciple of Jesus.[6]

In conclusion, Luke portrays the prayer of forgiveness as a decision. The decision to pray for one's persecutors is a choice to love them and to hope for their future conversion. It is an invitation that summons the power of God into the violent domain.

A Prayer Addressed to Another

As he did on the Mount of Olives, Jesus begins his prayer on the cross with the word "Father." That the Scriptures recount Jesus addressing God as "Father" is uncontested. Contemporary pastoral applications of the prayer of forgiveness may necessitate an address of God which is more inclusive.[7] The title was reminiscent of both the authority and the tenderness of God.[8] God is not merely the progenitor of the human race; Israel understands the fatherhood of God because of the experience of God's care and protection in its own salvation history.[9]

This God is the God who extends mercy even in the face of human ingratitude. The prophets constantly challenge Israel's lack of gratitude for its divine election. Unlike the unfaithful people, God's choice remains constant. In order to discipline them, God puts the chosen people to the test. In their misery the people cry out for forgiveness and mercy (Isa 63:15-19; 64). In response, God answers the pain of Israel with compassion and healing forgiveness (Hos 11:3, 8-9; Jer 3:22; 31:9, 20).

The Lucan Jesus speaks to God directly as "Father" (23:34, 46) and refers to God as "my Father" (2:49; 24:49). Jesus also teaches his disciples to call God "Father" (11:2). God is shown to be parental through knowing the needs of the disciples (12:30), responding generously to these needs (12:31), and giving the disciples the gift of the Holy Spirit (11:13). It is the will of the Father to give the disciples the Kingdom (12:32). Because God is faithful and providential, the disciples have no need to worry (12:29-32).[10]

Calling God one's Father means that one not only recognizes the invitation to familial relationship with God, but also acknowledges the obligation to form and let one's conduct be shaped through surrender to the divine will. Those who belong to this divine family are characterized by their willingness to do the will of God (Luke 8:21). They are kind to those who are ungrateful and wicked (Luke 6:35). Since God has shown them mercy, they deal mercifully with others (Luke 6:36).

To call God one's Father is to open oneself to conversion.[11] For the disciple, familial relationship with God is a journey toward holiness whose destiny is eschatological glory. The process by which one becomes a child of God is brought to perfection in the heavenly eschaton.[12] On the lips of Jesus the calling upon God as Father signals the presence of the eschatological age that is both present and coming. In Jesus human filial relationship is reestablished. This union presupposes perseverance through trial (Luke 22:28).

By choosing to pray the prayer of forgiveness, Jesus testifies, even in the moment of violence, that God is truly his Father and that his person and mission will be upheld and fulfilled by God. By this action Jesus hopes against hope in the eschatological fruitfulness of the will of God. Because Jesus understands God's faithfulness, he calls upon God even when all appearances mock God's fidelity. In a like manner Stephen, at the moment of death, asks Jesus to forgive and entrusts his spirit into the hands of the Lord Jesus (Acts 7:59-60).

One observes that neither Jesus nor Stephen looks upon his persecutors and says, "I forgive you." Rather, Jesus prays "Father, forgive them," and Stephen cries "Lord, do not hold this sin against them." Stephen, the model disciple, follows Jesus' example in praying for his persecutors.

To summarize, one notices that the prayer of forgiveness is a prayer addressed to another—to God. Christians do not rely on their own power to forgive their persecutors. Rather, because they trust and know deeply the power of God, Christians call upon God who alone is able to forgive. Because Christians trust deeply in God's providence, they know that, in spite of appearances which seem to indicate the contrary, God's generosity will not be undermined by evil.

A Prayer Petitioning Forgiveness

In Luke 4:18 the mission of Jesus is expressed as one that gives release—*aphesis*—to those who are oppressed. This release is considered as an experience of salvation. "'Release from sin is proclaimed at the inauguration of Jesus' mission (4:18), carried out in his acts of healing (e.g., 5:17-26) and given as a commission to the post-Easter community (24:47).'"[13] This release, as it is announced in Jesus' mission pronouncement, occurs after the proclamation that Jesus is sent to bring Good News to the poor. It includes those economically deprived and enslaved in debt.[14]

Jesus is called to release those in bondage of disease (Acts 10:38). Luke 5:17-26 describes the healing of the paralytic and contains the first reference to Jesus forgiving another of his sins. It is also Jesus' first encounter with the scribes and Pharisees and begins a series of controversies with them.[15] Although the story contains a miracle, its emphasis revolves around Jesus' power to forgive sins. The miracle confirms Jesus' authority over sin. Jesus is able to accomplish a work, the forgiveness of sins, that is the deed of God alone (Luke 5:21).[16]

Jesus incarnates his mission of forgiveness through association with sinners. He allies himself with tax collectors and sinners (Luke 5:27-31). Although sinners repent, which is the ingredient necessary for accepting the forgiveness of God, the scribes and self-righteous Pharisees fail to recognize their sinfulness (Luke 5:31-32). While Simon the Pharisee judges both the sinful woman and Jesus, Jesus, who is the friend of tax collectors and sinners, forgives the sins of the woman (Luke 7:36-50). When Zacchaeus, a tax collector, reforms his life and Jesus proclaims salvation to his household, the religious leaders grumble against Jesus (Luke 19:1-10).

One notices that the forgiveness of sins is an important motif in the Gospel of Luke not only because of its numerous occurrences, but also because of the schismatic nature of these occurrences. Throughout the narrative Jesus' power to forgive sins is accompanied not only by the joy, peace, gratitude, and conversion of the one saved, but also by the negative criticism of the scribes and Pharisees. Forgiving the enemy and the out-cast has social implications.[17]

In the Lucan corpus the invitation to repentance and the message of forgiveness in the name of Jesus are to be preached to all (Luke 24:47; Acts 1:8). Through acceptance of the message, the experience of salvation is open to Jew and Gentile alike. Unlike Israel who hoped in a salvation of the future, the Lucan corpus speaks of the experience of salvation through the forgiveness of sins as a reality realized, at least to some extent, in the present. "Today" (Luke 19:9; 23:43) is truly the day of salvation.[18] Yet Jesus' forgiveness of sins invites the experience of salvation for some and the experience of unbelief and hardheartedness for others. Some will have faith, while others will be unbelieving.

This theme of belief and unbelief associated with the experience of forgiveness and therefore of salvation is continued throughout the Acts of the Apostles. In Acts 4:4 many believe after Peter's speech, but Peter and John are held in custody by unbelieving religious leaders. Although many come to believe through the signs and wonders performed by the apostles in Jerusalem (5:12-16), the religious leaders jail them because of jealousy (5:17-18). In Acts 8:1-8 persecution of the faithful in Judea enables the acceptance of the faith in Samaria. Paul, as a true disciple of Jesus, experiences the same pattern of responses. At Antioch some will believe (13:44-47) while others will reject the message (13:50-51). The same happens at Thessalonika (17:2-4, 12; 17:5-9, 13) and at Corinth (18:7-11; 18:12-17).[19]

This same division can be observed after the prayer of forgiveness uttered by the crucified Jesus. While some soldiers jeer at Jesus (Luke 23:36-37), the centurion glorifies God and proclaims Jesus' innocence (23:47). While the people watch and return home beating their breasts (23:35, 48), the rulers mock the salvation brought by Jesus (23:35). While one thief believes in Jesus and obtains the promise of Paradise, the other thief sneers at Jesus' apparent inability to save himself (23:39-42).

Although Jesus teaches the disciples to pray that their sins might be forgiven (Luke 11:4), the prayer of confession of sins is conspicuously absent from the lips of Jesus[20] and Stephen. In the prayer of Jesus and of Stephen the petition is that the Father or Jesus might forgive the persecutors. Both Jesus and Stephen choose to petition God's saving forgiveness within the situation of evil, thereby inviting their murderers, through the power of God, to a new future.

It is God who releases the murderers from their sins. Because the oppressors are ignorant, it is the victim who begs God for forgiveness. This forgiveness and its consequent release from guilt invite the persecutors to repentance and offer them the opportunity of joining the Christian community. Although the community is affected by the evil inflicted on it by its oppressors, yet, through the power and creativity of God, it flourishes despite the occurrence of evil. The forgiving power of God, although rejected by some, cannot be conquered.

In conclusion, one observes that the forgiveness proclaimed by Jesus evokes both positive and negative responses. Those who accept the grace of forgiveness are invited into the Christian community. Those who reject this grace become the object of the prayer of the Christian community. It is through forgiveness that the person, as well as the entire human family, experiences salvation. Forgiveness, therefore, has social implications which are expressed and realized to the extent that the Church is faithful to its commission to pray for its persecutors.

An Excuse for the "Other":
"For they do not know what they are doing" (Luke 23:34)

Who is the "they" of the prayer of forgiveness? There are many, including the soldiers armed with swords, the disciples armed with swords, Peter whom Jesus' glance catches with words of denial on his lips, and Judas armed with a money bag and a kiss, who have betrayed Jesus. All are somewhat responsible for what has transpired.

Through Jesus' prayer of forgiveness, Luke illustrates the unconditional mercy of God that is to be expressed concretely in the lives of true disciples. Union with God's will and participation in God's glory are possible only through the disciples' willingness to forgive. Rudolf Bultmann claims that "God's forgiveness is not deduced from an idea of God or His grace, but is experienced as His act in the event of salvation, so that preaching does not consist in illuminating instruction regarding the idea of God but in the proclamation of the act of God."[21] This willingness to forgive one's persecutors is the key to the eschatological kingdom which is already begun in and through the Church.[22]

The growth of the Church depends on the persistence of Christians in praying for those who persecute them. The conversion and apostolic mission of Saul is one striking example of this phenomenon. The conversion of a former oppressor of the Christian community and acceptance of him into the ranks of those personally afflicted by the former persecutor's violence prompts suspicion and fear (Acts 9:13-14, 26). In order for the Christian community to grow and to flourish, forgiveness needs to be exercised by God and also practically and painfully by the community. Early Christians were challenged to accept those who persecuted family and friends as brothers and sisters in Christ. The misguided past of the newfound believer needed to be put to rest by means of the excuse of unwitting ignorance.[23]

The request for forgiveness on the grounds of ignorance is a theme known in Latin, Greek, and Jewish literature.[24] In the case of Jesus' petition on the grounds of innocence, one might wonder whom Luke specifically intended as the object of this prayer.[25] If Jesus is praying for the Romans, the sense would be that these soldiers are ignorant because they have not had the opportunity to hear the gospel. If Jesus is praying for the Jews, it means that the Jews have not understood the meaning of Jesus' message. The self-righteousness of the Jewish leaders (Luke 18:10-12) blinds their perception. Their characterization of themselves and of Jesus is false. Because of their false speculations, the Jewish leaders feel justified in their unloving, exclusive, and unmerciful judgments. The presence of Jesus brings them the spirit of confusion. They are filled with awe because of him (Luke 5:26) and yet murmur against him (Luke 15:2).[26] While the Romans lack information, the Jews lack understanding.[27]

Early legal and ethical systems recognize the mitigating circumstance of inadequate information. An early scriptural example is found in Genesis 20. Here Abimelech, because he is ignorant of the fact that Sarah belongs to Abraham, is freed from death for the crime of taking Abraham's wife. Indulgence, however, for those who err through lack of understanding is a relatively late ethical phenomenon.[28] The New Testament writers struggle with this issue. Why is it that those who seemingly had every advantage could not understand the Gospel of Jesus? Is it because God does not grant them understanding (Mark 4:12)? Is God guilty of blinding their hearts and their minds (John 12:40)? Is the one who is ignorant of the will of God less guilty than the one who has been enlightened (Luke 12:47-48)? Is ignorance simply part of the human condition (Heb 5:2)?

Experientially the distinctions between the excuse by reason of ignorance and the excuse by reason of lack of understanding are not always clear. Those who are ignorant often are so because they lack understanding. Those who lack understanding do so because they are in many respects ignorant. Education is not necessarily salvation. One can plead naïveté for those persecutors who are convinced that they are right and who prove this conviction by neither concealing nor censoring the atrocities of their crimes. Naive persecutors truly do not know what they are doing.[29]

The second half of Jesus' prayer is not echoed in the prayer of Stephen.[30] Conzelmann posits that "complementary to this allowance for ignorance, there is, of course, the positive declaration that now, after the revelation, that is, after the Resurrection, there is no more excuse; the times of ignorance which God overlooked are now past."[31] Although this theory might explain the absence of the ignorance motif in the account of the martyrdom of Stephen, it fails to consider the repetition of this motif in Eusebius's account of the martyrdom of James and also the motif's consistent recurrence throughout the Acts of the Apostles. The evidence suggests that excusing the enemy because the enemy is ignorant is key to understanding Christian discipleship. This leniency for the purpose of inviting the enemy to conversion was the task not only of the earthly Jesus but is also the task of the post-resurrectional Church. Even after the resurrection, ignorance, as demonstrated throughout the Acts of the Apostles, is a fact of life.

The Lucan relationship between forgiveness and ignorance is found throughout the Acts of the Apostles.[32] After curing the cripple, Peter addresses those assembled and, because of their ignorance, excuses the crowd as well as their leaders for the death of Jesus (Acts 3:17). In the synagogue at Antioch in Pisidia, Paul absolves the people of Jerusalem and their leaders of the death of Jesus because they failed to recognize him (13:27). Gentiles, through the preaching of the gospel, are now free to repent of their ignorance (17:30).

All are included in the prayer of forgiveness. The Christian community is to imitate the mercy of God and the example of Jesus in praying for and loving the oppressor. Luke uses a diverse cast of characters to demonstrate this point. The criminal on the cross is immediately promised forgiveness and Paradise (Luke 23:43). The prayer of forgiveness brings forth fruit in the reaction of the Roman centurion who proclaims Jesus' innocence (Acts 23:47). When the people who gathered to watch the crucifixion are blessed by the prayer of forgiveness, they return home beating their breasts in repentance.[33]

The reader of Luke first meets this crowd outside the Jerusalem temple while Zechariah prays within (Luke 1:10). The angel prophesies that it will be the role of John to prepare a people who are fit for the Lord (1:17). At the cross the people contemplate Jesus who appears unable to save himself, let alone them (23:35). Yet, the repentant thief is the first to call on the Lord's name (Luke 23:42; Acts 2:21; 4:12; 8:12; 9:21). He is also the first to receive forgiveness of sins through this name (Luke 23:43; Acts 10:43; 22:16). Meanwhile, the crowds beat their breasts, foreshadowing what will become the repentance necessary to appropriate the Pentecostal event (Acts 2:38).[34]

For Luke, praying for forgiveness is essential to the Christian life. Because God has forgiven them, Christians are able to participate in divine life. In order to realize this life of the Spirit in the context of the Christian community, the disciples of Jesus must pray for those who persecute them. Forgiveness is central to the Christian experience of salvation. The experience of Christian salvation is known both from being forgiven and from praying the prayer of forgiveness (Luke 6:35-36).[35]

Those who are self-righteous and lack understanding are perhaps the most difficult to forgive. While hanging on the cross, Jesus does not continue to preach repentance to the self-righteous. Rather, Jesus prays for their forgiveness on the grounds that they truly do not know what they are doing. Forgiveness is effective only for those who have faith (Luke 5:20; 7:48-50). For the rest Jesus must pray and trust in the mercy of his Father.

Luke does not present the Jewish religious leaders as evil, as does Matthew (Matt 9:4; 12:34; 16:4), but rather as foolish (Luke 11:40). They have taken the key of knowledge, but they have not used this key for either themselves or for others (Luke 11:52). Although their stubbornness causes Jesus great pain (19:41-44), Jesus refuses to condemn them. Rather, he repeatedly speaks the truth to them and prays for their forgiveness. Luke leaves the door of repentance open to those who are self-righteous. Jesus demonstrates that his love includes even those whose foolishness, despite their every advantage, frustrates and attempts to destroy his life and mission. Jesus does not desire to shatter his persecutors, but to love and forgive them.[36]

In conclusion, it can be seen that although the Christian prayer of forgiveness is offered for all, it can be effective only when, as demonstrated by the two thieves, it is received with a repentant heart. Since repentance is always possible, the Christian is called to both pray for the persecutor and excuse the persecutor on the grounds of ignorance. This is done for two reasons. First, prayer for the persecutor and excusing the persecutor allow the oppressor the freedom to choose conversion. Because retaliatory violence, which locks people into a defensive posture, is not accepted, conversion becomes a real option even if it is not always the option people choose. Second, the prayer and excuse for the oppressor invite the persecutor out of the cold hate of violence into a community of love. Not only can persecutors choose conversion, but upon choosing it they are welcomed, at least in the ideal Lucan community, as a friend.

The Second Dynamic

"Father, into your hands I commend my spirit" (Luke 23:46)

"Lord Jesus, receive my spirit" (Acts 7:59)

The last words of Jesus, "Father, into your hands I commend my spirit" (Luke 23:46), are an echo of Psalm 31:5. A number of such parallels exist between texts from Old Testament wisdom literature and the Lucan passion narrative.[37] Psalm 31 begins with an expression of fundamental trust in the fidelity of God. In the prayer on the Mount of Olives and the prayer of request for forgiveness on the cross, Jesus also begins with the address, "Father." The prefacing of the prayer of surrender with this formal address and the change of the verb from *parathesomai* ("I will commit") to *paratithemai* ("I commit") are two alterations Luke makes in the psalmist's prayer. Although some scholars understand the verbal alteration as insignificant, Frank Matera argues for the theological significance of both changes. Both emphasize Jesus' union with the Father and his dedication to accomplishing the divine will. Entrusting his spirit to the Father is accomplished as a present reality rather than an ongoing decision open to a definitive future. Jesus can still call God his Father because until the end he continues to do the Father's will. By addressing his prayer to the Father, Jesus is declaring once again that he is truly Son of God.[38]

The Father who has entrusted all things to Jesus (Luke 10:22) now receives the spirit of his Son. The Lucan Jesus who trusted in the will of the Father throughout his life, dies with a prayer of trust on his lips (Luke 23:46). This account of the prayer of Jesus at the time of death differs significantly from the account in Mark. In the Gospel of Mark, Jesus is silent from the time of his words to Pilate (15:2) until he utters the opening line of Psalm 22 on the cross (15:34). The Markan Jesus dies with a wordless scream (15:37).[39]

In contrast, the Lucan Jesus expires with the words of Psalm 31:5 on his lips.[40] Jesus truly is the one who from the beginning until the end perseveres in prayer. The power of darkness even at the moment of Jesus' death does not have the power to extinguish Jesus' persistent prayerful conversation with his Father. The Greek word describing Jesus' last breath is *exepneusen,* meaning "He gave out his spirit." Death does not rob Jesus of his life; rather, Jesus in full authority surrenders his spirit into the hands of the Father.[41]

In his study of Jesus' dying prayer in Mark and in Luke, Frank Matera suggests that Luke, rather than obtaining his information from another source, is editing the Markan source. Mark places an emphasis on the abandonment of Jesus. After being abandoned by his hometown (Mark 6:1-6) and his disciples (14:43-46, 50, 66-72), Jesus is abandoned even by God (15:34). Psalm 22 as an expression of this abandonment is in line with Mark's theme.[42]

On the other hand, Luke's objective is to portray Jesus as the one who willingly undertakes the task of accomplishing the divine will of God. This task is accomplished through perfect trust in and obedience to the divine will of the Father. Mark's cry of dereliction does not comply with such an objective. Because it succinctly focuses Luke's theme, Psalm 31:5 seems to be the better choice. Jesus who has faithfully done the Father's will now dies trusting in this same Father.[43]

Note that Psalms 22 and 31 each contain both the theme of abandonment and of trust. Psalm 22, although beginning with the theme of abandonment, also expresses trust in God (see vv. 5, 24, 31). Psalm 31, although proposing radical trust in God (vv. 5, 14), also expresses abandonment (vv. 9-13, 22). The psalmist in both cases experiences apparent abandonment by God and yet, in the midst of this distress, the faith of the psalmist enables trust in God's providence.[44]

At the moment of death, Jesus hands his spirit over to the Father. Several times in the gospel, Jesus has been handed over into the clutches of those who have persecuted him (Luke 9:44; 18:32; 20:19; 22:53; 24:7). The exodus which was to be accomplished in Jerusalem is now complete. Jesus' mission is fulfilled. The angels had long ago promised peace to those who are favored by God (Luke 2:14). Those who make the decision to obey the will of God as Jesus has will find peace amid the reality of persecution. Because Jesus has fulfilled the way ordained by the Father, he is able to die in peace.[45]

The time of darkness is conquered by Jesus' persistent prayer. Even when all is dark and evil seems to have the upper hand, Jesus hands over his spirit, confident in the fidelity and power of God. "Now his *exodus* was completed and he would return to God in order to lavish on the world the Spirit of forgiveness and salvation."[46] The prayer commending one's spirit to the hands of God is for Luke not just another prayer but the culminating prayer. In it the battle against the violence of the evil spirit is won. Jesus dies with a prayer of forgiveness on his lips and in peaceful trust in his Father.[47]

Stephen dies with a vision which affirms Jesus' resurrected victory over evil and therefore Stephen's vindication. His prayer of surrender is addressed to Jesus. Stephen sees the Son of God, Jesus, standing at the right hand of God and prays to him. This vision fulfills Jesus' prophecy made during his own trial (Luke 22:69). The words of Stephen are proved true through this theophany. This faithful disciple needs only to echo the words of Jesus and thus be faithful unto death.[48]

Since readers have been told that Stephen is a man filled with the Holy Spirit, as was Mary (Luke 1:35), John the Baptist (Luke 1:15), Elizabeth (Luke 1:41), and Zechariah (Luke 1:67), they know that Stephen acts and speaks the words of God. The transfiguration of Stephen (Acts 6:15) further signals that the words of Stephen are in line with the will and Spirit of God.

Jesus thus becomes the mediator and the advocate for Christians under persecution. He is the one that Christians can pray to in order to intercede for their persecutors. They can address their prayer to Jesus in the same way that Jesus addressed his prayer to the Father. Luke proclaims Jesus' identity with God and with God's mission. Now that Jesus is at the right hand of the power of God, Christians can ask him what they previously could petition only from God.[49]

Prayer addressed to Jesus may be foreshadowed in Luke's Gospel by words addressed to Jesus. The petitions, "Jesus, Master, have mercy on us" (17:13), "Jesus, Son of David, have mercy on me" (18:38), and "Son of David, have mercy on me" (18:39) point to that which was to follow. Stephen, the man filled with the Holy Spirit, is the first to explicitly address his prayer to Jesus.[50] This prayer echoes, with the exception of its christological address, the words of the persecuted Jesus.[51]

Some authors suggest that the prayer of surrendering one's spirit was perhaps, at least in later Judaism, a traditional evening prayer.[52] Whether or not this custom was in place at the time of Luke or, if it was in place is implicitly referred to here by Luke, is not clear. Bock, although recognizing that "Psalm 31 may have been a common prayer in the Jewish community since it appears to have been used by the pious as a frequent evening prayer as it calls on God to watch over his saints," also admits that "the evidence for this use is late, so care is needed in citing it. It could reflect the accessibility of Psalm 31 for this context." Moreover, Bock posits that the Lucan prayer of surrender might correspond to the second cry of Mark and have its origin in a supplementary Passion source.[53]

Since the prayer evokes images of childlike trust and confidence in God,[54] its effect in the narrative is to invite into the hour of darkness and violence an atmosphere of stability and serenity. Jesus' authority is rooted in the power of the Holy Spirit (Luke 4:18-21). Jesus surrenders this spirit not to the mockery of evil, but into the hands of his Father. Although it has stripped him of all else, evil cannot abduct from Jesus the Holy Spirit of God. Jesus does not curse the human agents of evil; rather, he hands his spirit to his Father and begs for forgiveness for those robbing him of life.

Jerome Neyrey understands Jesus' prayer of surrender in terms of the leitmotif of "faith saves." The theme of faith saving someone is found throughout Luke's Gospel (7:50; 8:48, 50; 17:19; 18:42). In the Acts of the Apostles this theme is reiterated. Those who call upon the Lord's name are saved (2:21). Christians are identified as those who call upon "the name" (9:14, 21; 22:16). Faith in the name of the Lord Jesus is a power that has the capacity to perform miracles (3:6, 16; 4:10). It is through faith in the name that forgiveness of sins is possible (10:43).[55]

In the Acts of the Apostles God is presented as the one who fulfills promises in Jesus. Jesus is the fulfillment of the promises made to Abraham and David. Accepting Jesus brings forgiveness and salvation. Because he persevered through his death in faith in the God who saves, Jesus is able to bring about salvation. Jesus promises the crucified criminal paradise and reaffirms his belief in life after death. Jesus, therefore, is a faithful believer in the God who is able to raise him from the dead. In predicting his passion Jesus speaks not only about his death but also about his resurrection (Luke 9:22; 18:33; 22:69; 23:43, 46; 24:7, 26, 44-46).[56]

In summary, one observes that Jesus and Stephen hand their spirits over in trust and confidence. It is this final act of faith that truly invites the salvific power of the Holy Spirit into the realm of violence. In order that the power of God might bring one's vocational mission to its fulfillment, one hands over one's spirit not to the power of evil, but back to God. Surrendering one's spirit enables God to vindicate the martyr's life and mission and invites the power of the Spirit into the Church. After praying that God will forgive, one must trust in God and hand over one's vocational mission into God's hands. Therefore, although humans can invite the power of God into the realm of violence, it is truly God who saves.

The Third Dynamic

The Manifestation of God's Fidelity

If prayer is a relational dynamic, one observes not only the prayer of the Christian but also the response of God. In this regard Luke demonstrates the prayer of forgiveness as an efficacious prayer. After Jesus prays the prayer of forgiveness, the criminal crucified with Jesus asks to be remembered in the kingdom (Luke 23:42). Jesus responds by promising that he would be with Jesus that day in Paradise (23:43). The invitation to repentance implicit in the prayer of forgiveness bears fruit in the Roman centurion who praises God and declares Jesus' innocence (23:47). E. Earle Ellis suggests that the centurion is "perhaps intended to prefigure the conversion of the Gentiles."[57] The people around the cross return home beating their breasts (23:48) and thus demonstrate the repentance needed for the appropriation of the grace of forgiveness. The efficacy of the repentance invited by the prayer of forgiveness is manifested by the mass Pentecostal conversions (Acts 2:41; 4:4).[58] Saul, who witnesses the martyrdom of Stephen and consents to the deed (Acts 22:20), seeks and receives the forgiveness of God already prayed for by Stephen. No one is excluded from the grace of the prayer of forgiveness.[59] To pray for those who abuse one (Luke 6:28) is to facilitate their conversion. This prayer for the oppressor is in fact a decision to love one's neighbor.

In the case of Stephen, Stephen's persecutors fulfill Gamaliel's prophetic words (Acts 5:39). In killing Stephen they are opposing the work of God. God's will, however, is not defeated.[60] Rather the very actions of those opposing God's work are the catalyst which propels the proclamation of the gospel far beyond what a living Stephen could have done. Stephen, filled with the Holy Spirit (Acts 6:3, 5), has spoken the living and active word of God.[61] This word, once spoken, is effective.[62] Stephen who surrenders his spirit into the hands of God can do so knowing that God will fulfill his life and his mission in ways beyond all imagining.[63]

In investigating the response of God to the prayer of the faithful Lucan disciple, two key elements must be wrestled with. First, the prayer of the faithful disciple will be answered in accordance with the divine will of God. This will of God is not cold and calculating, but rather promises salvation to those who embrace it.[64] As it was for Jesus, the vindication and glorification of the disciple is accomplished through obedience to the divine *dei* (Acts 5:29; 9:6, 16; 14:22; 19:21; 20:35; 23:11; 27:24). Second, the response of God to the prayer of the persecuted one is effective in creative and surprising ways,[65] but it does not usher in the definitive parousia. The disciple experiences the fulfillment of some eschatological promises in the present, but also realizes that the message of the gospel is not fully accepted by the human family. Because many are either ignorant or lack understanding, they are incapable of accepting the gospel message.

Norman Perrin interprets Luke 17:20-21 by suggesting that even though the presence of the parousia is not definitely accomplished, historical events present to human experience signal that the kingdom is in some sense present: sins are forgiven, demonic power is broken, sinners are gathered into communion with God. However, to experience the kingdom "among you" (Luke 17:21), one must have the faith needed to interpret events rightly and to commit oneself to the work of the kingdom. Since the Christian lives in the eschatological tension between the present and the future, this faith presupposes ethical responsibility. The Lucan Christian learns from the example of Jesus how to address God as *Father* and receives the ethical command to forgive the enemy.[66]

John T. Carroll suggests that when dealing with the now and not yet presence of the kingdom of God, as this is presented in the Lucan corpus, it is of more value "to focus on the theme of fulfillment of promise in the present, rather than on the presence of the kingdom. A set of (eschatological) promises already fulfilled provides reassurance that as yet unfulfilled promises will have their day."[67]

As evident from the deaths of both Jesus and Stephen, prayer does not always save the disciple from immediate harm.[68] Although the disciples are told to pray that they might be saved from the test, they are also given the example of Jesus and Stephen, to surrender their spirits into the hands of the Father when evil seems to take the upper hand. Thus, although the accomplishment of the will of God seems to take precedence at times over the very lives of the disciples, if they remain faithful to prayer and persistent in following the will of God, the disciples' lives and missions will ultimately be fulfilled. This ultimate fulfillment is signed through salvific action which, although not fully realized, already begins to bear fruit "today."

Although the death of a disciple will not usher in the fullness of eschatological victory, signs that God's kingdom is at hand will break in immediately.[69] Jesus' persistence in prayer bears fruit in the repentance of the good thief. Stephen's prayer introduces the Gentile mission.

Not only will God confirm the mission and life of the disciple, but in order to accomplish this confirmation, God will grace the deeds of one's very persecutors.[70] This is possible because prayer invites the power of God into the realm of darkness. This power of God has a double effect. For those able to accept the message, this power of the Spirit of God inspires repentance, conversion, and baptism. For those who are bound in ignorance, the presence of the Spirit prompts further persecution. Christian hope, however, is undaunted. As long as the oppressors are able to persecute, they also possess the potential for conversion.

Simeon foreshadowed this acceptance/rejection theme by prophesying that Jesus would be the cause of the fall and the rise of many in Israel (Luke 2:34). Because of the example of Jesus and Stephen, the Christian knows that the evil of persecution itself will result, albeit in surprising and creative ways, in the continuance and further spread of the gospel. Since to do the will of God is the ultimate desire and joy of the martyr, the martyr's mission and fulfillment cannot be destroyed by the attack of evil. If the disciples live, it is to continue to be faithful to the mission of the gospel. If the disciples die, they surrender their spirits into the hands of the Father who alone is able to validate and fulfill their vocational missions.[71] Like Jesus, it is obedience to the divine "must" of one's own life, an identity only discovered through persistent prayer, which is able to bring one the freedom of salvation and is able to further the realization of the kingdom of God on earth.

Luke's focus is not on who is to be blamed for a particular crime or on the earthly betterment brought to a person or persons because they heard and believed the gospel. Rather, he suggests that when the disciple discerns the will of God, follows it in obedience, and dies because of this vocational mission, the Church as representative of the kingdom of God will grow in fervor and number. Success in the realization of the kingdom is not equated with political victory, economic relief, or improved social status. However, the advancement of the kingdom of God, because it forgives and excuses the persecutor thus making it possible for persecutors to open themselves to the possibility of conversion,[72] invites political changes, economic reform, and respect for the dignity of all people. Jesus is not a political Messiah, but his mission focused on the will of God does have, especially where the will of God is blocked by violence, political consequences. These political consequences are not necessarily advantageous to the Christian community. If prayer for the forgiveness of the persecutor is persistent, it will result in the conversion of some, intensified persecution by others, and further evangelization.

According to the Lucan witness, salvation is experienced through the forgiveness of sins.[73] This forgiveness is freely given by God, is manifested in Jesus' dealings with sinners, and is effective in those disposed toward receiving it. The experience of salvation through the forgiveness of one's sins, however, is known only by those who are willing to forgive (Luke 7:36-49; 15:11-24; 18:9-14).[74]

The prayer of forgiveness recognizes the need for prayers of intercession and petition in the age of the Church. That God answers petitionary prayer is affirmed early in the Lucan Gospel. Zechariah, because God has heard his petition, will be blessed with a son (Luke 1:13). The Lord's prayer, while acknowledging the priority of the kingdom of God, petitions for the realization of true human community and for practical human needs. Presented as the model prayer for the Christian, the Lord's prayer is made up of a series of five petitions requesting the satisfaction of both spiritual and temporal needs (Luke 11:2-4).[75]

In the Acts of the Apostles the result of petitionary prayer is also demonstrated. Prayerful waiting for the Holy Spirit results in the Pentecostal demonstration of God's power. As a consequence of this prayer three thousand were incorporated into the early Church (2:41). Cornelius the centurion prays (10:1-4) and as a result Peter receives enlightenment concerning the baptism of Gentiles (10:9-29, 44-48). When Peter is confined to prison, the Church prays earnestly for him (12:5). The petition of the Church is answered in Peter's miraculous escape (12:6-17). When the apostle Paul asks the Lord what he should do, the Lord reveals to him the next step he is to take in his life (22:10). To call on the Lord's name in prayer is so characteristic of Luke's ecclesiology that it becomes the identifying mark of what it means to be a Christian (Acts 2:21; 7:59; 9:14, 21; 22:16).[76]

Prayer is "the means by which the dynamic energy of the Spirit is apprehended."[77] In the Gospel of Luke Jesus tells his disciples that there are two things the Father has a desire to give them. First, it is the Father's pleasure to bestow upon them the kingdom (Luke 12:32). Second, the Father wants to give the Holy Spirit to those who ask (Luke 11:13). There is indeed a connection between prayer, the kingdom, and the Holy Spirit.

Prayer is the means by which the disciple becomes subject to the influence of the Holy Spirit and, therefore, the Holy Spirit is the principle answer to the disciple's prayer (Luke 3:21-22; 11:13; Acts 4:31; 8:15; 13:1-4). It is significant that Luke modifies his source insisting not that the heavenly Father will give "good gifts" to those who ask, but rather that the heavenly Father will give "the Holy Spirit" to those who ask (Luke 11:13).[78] The sign of this Spirit is the authority and power of the kingdom of God already present in Jesus and continued in the Church.[79]

The kingdom of God is formed through the preaching of the gospel through the power of the Holy Spirit. This authoritative preaching is not possible until the disciples are given the free gift of the Holy Spirit of God. Once given this Spirit, the disciples are to preach repentance for the forgiveness of sins through baptism in the name of Jesus (Luke 24:47).[80] As in the case of Jesus, the gospel message proclaimed by the disciples is received by some and rejected by others.

To summarize, one observes that for Luke petitionary prayer is the means through which the power of the Spirit, inaugurating the forgiveness of sins as a salvific event, is able to break into the world. The presence of the Holy Spirit signs the presence of the kingdom of God. The Pentecostal Church, filled with the power of the Holy Spirit through the life and death of Jesus, mediates the presence of the kingdom of God in history.[81] Jesus, in accordance with the will of the Father, is addressed through the petitionary prayer of the disciple and, with the Father, dispenses the gift of the Holy Spirit upon those who ask (Luke 11:13; 24:49; Acts 1:4-5).

A Summary of the Lucan Dynamics

Jesus and Stephen respond to violence in a paradigmatic way. What does their example say to Christians who are struggling to forgive those who have injured them? What practical elements do Christians need to appropriate in order that they may truly forgive?

The Lucan prayer of forgiveness suggests several elements that pastoral helpers might consider as they attempt to guide victims along the way toward Christian forgiveness. First, it is obvious that the Lucan victim decides to forgive because the victim, at least to some degree, understands God's unconditional love and wishes to love others in the same way. Even though Christian victims suffer from the injustice perpetrated, they are motivated to forgive because they have experienced God's unconditional love. If disciples are truly in love with the Holy Spirit of God, they must choose this Spirit of love and of truth not only within the confines of prayer, but also in relationship to their neighbors.

Second, the power to forgive does not come from oneself. The Christian, as a child of God, addresses the prayer of forgiveness to the Father or to Jesus and experiences the power of this forgiveness in the surprising action of the Holy Spirit. Realizing it is the power of God that has the capacity to make all things new, Christian victims know they must invite this power of God into situations of conflict.

Third, Christians forgive in order to offer their persecutors a future that contains possibilities for conversion. Because Christians refuse to enslave their persecutors in categories of hatred that bind and segregate, Christians, even as their persecutors are doing all they can to destroy this invitation, continue to reach out in love. The prayer of forgiveness, therefore, plays out the ethical imperative of doing the truth in love. Christians, motivated by the love of Christ, speak the truth to those who have hardened hearts. As a result of this bold, yet loving action, Christians make themselves vulnerable to possible, even likely, retaliation from those whose hearts are hardened. If Christians do become victims of this retaliation, they continue through the prayer of forgiveness to hold out to the perpetrator the possibility of future conversion.

Fourth, the Christian dynamic of forgiveness is not obsessed with assessing blame. It does not allow itself to become entangled in the web of deceit and intrigue. Rather, its focus is on God and one's relationship with God as expressed through love

of neighbor. Although the Christian will insist on propheti-
cally speaking the truth to those who are deceived, in the moment of violence Christians, conscious that they too have been
forgiven, witness to the truth through their prayer of forgiveness.

Fifth, the prayer of forgiveness, while acknowledging the
pain of violence, also acknowledges the truth of the situation.
Those perpetrating the violence do so either because they lack
the facts, or because they have failed to integrate and therefore
to understand the facts. Acknowledging that the offense of the
perpetrator stems from this ignorance or lack of understanding helps the Christian to pray fervently for those who have
not had the blessing of either hearing or of understanding the
gospel. Christian victims do not hold their persecutors in contempt for their lack of understanding. Rather, followers of
Jesus realize that their understanding is a gift of God and wish
only to continue to invite the other in order that the other
might also receive this gift.

Sixth, the prayer of forgiveness has both an active and a passive dimension. Christians struggling in situations riveted
with violence can make the decision to pray and to persevere
in prayer for their persecutors. If the violence subsides, they
can resume their work in proclaiming the gospel, in doing the
deeds of justice, and in daily praying for those who injure
them (Luke 6:28; 11:4). If the violence ends in death or in the
blocking of their continuance in the mission, faithful Christians can choose to entrust their spirits into the hands of God.
In short, Christians must be detached from whether their mission of proclaiming the gospel results in life or in death, in success or in failure. Their mission is a gift of God. If they dedicate
their lives to the love of God and to the mission of the gospel,
they must trust that ultimately it is God who will resurrect and
fulfill their lives and missions.

Seventh, those praying the prayer of forgiveness hope that
God will answer their prayer. They know that although they
might give up their lives for the sake of the gospel, God will
fulfill their lives and missions beyond all expectation.

While acknowledging these seven elements, the theologian
pondering contemporary pastoral situations is aware that the

situational dimensions of the Lucan prayer of forgiveness cannot be strictly paralleled with situations of clients who might approach a contemporary pastoral counselor. One must consider that Jesus and Stephen, although victims of violence, are victims precisely because of their vocational mission. Neither Jesus nor Stephen is, for example, a victim of random violence. Neither is a victim of childhood abuse. Neither is persecuted specifically because of race, gender, economic status, etc. Therefore, when presenting the prayer of forgiveness as a paradigm for Christian forgiveness and applying this to contemporary cases, one cannot simplistically claim that all situations requiring forgiveness are the same.

Likewise, neither Jesus nor Stephen physically survives the violent attack. Both die as a consequence of the abuse. Both experience their violation as adults. What might their example say, therefore, to those who must live with the consequences of survival? What do their lives offer the living victim who is challenged to forgive a violator who has died? What might the Lucan paradigm say to Christians who were violated as children?

It is obvious from these preliminary questions that, in order to interpret the Lucan prayer of forgiveness in a way that might speak to contemporary victims, further reflection is needed. Pastoral theologians, often faced with their own clients' inability to forgive, have offered various approaches designed to enable Christian victims to advance their own healing by means of Christian forgiveness. These approaches attempt to interpret the scriptural message of forgiveness in a way that is both appropriate and meaningful to contemporary victims. This study will continue by examining these theologies in order to facilitate dialogue between pastoral theology and the Lucan prayer of forgiveness.

4

Answering Contemporary Questions: The Contribution of Pastoral Theology

Wading Through the Literature

Recent popular and scholarly literature includes numerous studies concerning psychological theories of forgiveness.[1] Studies utilizing the insights and techniques of various therapeutic schools to help clients seek forgiveness are available.[2] Existing literature has shown forgiveness to be relevant to the healing of hurts created by such diverse problems as sexual assault, divorce, gerontological concerns, depression, bulimia, abortion, agoraphobia, compulsivity, sexual misbehavior, anger, and interpersonal relationships in general.[3]

The goal of this chapter is to examine current counseling literature on forgiveness which seeks to base itself in the Christian tradition. In bibliographies of professional periodical articles and of dissertations attempting to integrate Christian theologies of forgiveness with psychological theories, works of five pastoral authors are cited most frequently: David Augsburger, *Caring Enough to Forgive: True Forgiveness* and *Caring Enough To Not Forgive: False Forgiveness,* which is really one work dedicating half of its content to each side of the discussion; Doris Donnelly, *Learning to Forgive* and *Putting Forgiveness into Practice;* Dennis Linn and Matthew Linn, *Healing*

Life's Hurts: Healing Memories through the Five Stages of Forgiveness; John Patton, *Is Human Forgiveness Possible?: A Pastoral Care Perspective;* and Lewis B. Smedes, *Forgive and Forget: Healing the Hurts We Don't Deserve.*[4]

David Augsburger

Augsburger's book, *Caring Enough To Forgive: True Forgiveness* and *Caring Enough To Not Forgive: False Forgiveness* focuses on the need for interpersonal reconciliation in the forgiveness process. "The real work of forgiving is not just the release from hatred, resentment, suspicion, and hostility in the forgiver, it is found in regaining the sister and brother as a full sister, as a true brother."[5] Since the community of persons is the image of God, one is in relationship with others in order to express this communion.[6] The principle, "forgiveness is necessary, reconciliation is optional," is not, according to Augsburger, based on the example of Jesus.[7] A forgiveness focused on release for one's own conscience instead of on the restoration of community is not truly Christian. "The goal is community restored, not private perfection maintained."[8]

Doris Donnelly

In her book, *Learning To Forgive,* Donnelly stresses the necessity of strategic timing in the forgiveness process. Reconciliation is only possible when forgiveness is allowed time to work. Not allowing oneself the time needed to confront, face, and work through one's hurts might speed the goal of reconciliation, but will not assure its quality.[9] Proposing that there is no sure strategy for the pursuit of reconciliation with another, Donnelly insists that no matter what the strategy, it must be motivated by love of the other.[10]

Dennis Linn and Matthew Linn

The Linns begin their book *Healing Life's Hurts: Healing Memories through the Five Stages of Forgiveness* with the thesis that painful memories can do one of two things: they can either cripple one throughout one's life or they can become one's gifts. Each event in one's life can be understood either as a blessing or a curse.[11]

Like physical wounds, emotional wounds heal gradually. The Linns posit that the healing of painful memories follows Elizabeth Kübler-Ross's five stages of death and dying: denial, anger, bargaining, depression, and acceptance.[12] In prayerfully processing the healing of memories, one moves from stage to stage, but also penetrates each stage at ever-greater depths. The five stages of this prayerful healing of wounds point to the natural way the Spirit heals.[13]

John Patton

In his work, *Is Human Forgiveness Possible?*, John Patton contends that when conceptualizing forgiveness as an act or attitude, many Christian clients, in spite of their best efforts, seem unable to forgive. Patton conceives of forgiveness not as a human act or attitude but as a discovery of a gift already given by God.[14] While shame is a response to rejection and frustration and as such encourages the client to build protective defenses, Patton's proposed therapeutic relationship offers the client the opportunity to explore the defenses of shame, e.g., rage, power, and righteousness, within an empathetic context in order to discover guilt.[15] Once one understands oneself as guilty, then one can recognize oneself as belonging to a community of sinners loved by God.[16] The pastoral counselor's role is not to supervise and encourage acts or attitudes of forgiveness, but to provide an appropriate empathetic atmosphere which enables a client to shed the defenses of shame and discover relatedness with others.[17]

Lewis Smedes

Smedes, in *Forgive and Forget: Healing the Hurts We Don't Deserve*, warns that false forgiving eventually corrodes the moral fiber of a society. He suggests that what is needed is "redemptive remembering," whereby one does not forget the past but focuses on hope-filled and redemptive future possibilities. Forgiving, since it is grounded in reality rather than in deception, does not fear confrontation, and is guided by a freedom stronger than hate. Forgiveness as "love's revolution against life's unfairness"[18] is guided by respect for the other and commitment to the other. It provides insight into the realization that no person is totally pure. One forgives because one realizes that God has forgiven the evil in one's own heart. Not to forgive one's neighbor, therefore, is a dishonest denial of the mixture of good and evil in every human heart.[19]

Implicit in each of these pastoral theories is a working theology of the nature of forgiveness, a pastoral theory concerning the process of forgiveness, and a pastoral hypothesis concerning the outcome of forgiveness, especially as this affects relationship with one's perpetrator. Dialogue with the pastoral authors will therefore proceed through the use of three questions: (1) What is Christian forgiveness?, which probes each author's understanding of forgiveness as a theological concept; (2) How does the Christian forgive?, which explores each author's recommended process of forgiveness; and (3) What is the relationship between forgiveness and reconciliation?, which examines the proposed outcome of each theory.

What Is Christian Forgiveness?

Understanding what forgiveness is requires that one separate true forgiveness from its aberrations. This theme of distinguishing true from false forgiveness is so prominent in the literature that it seems wise to follow the lead of pastoral theologians in making this differentiation before investigating their descriptions of true Christian forgiveness.

David Augsburger labels as counterfeit a forgiveness that takes a morally superior position.[20] He goes so far as to label most unilateral forgiveness as false forgiveness. Although some situations of violence may require one-way forgiveness, most interpersonal conflicts will require reconciliation between parties in order to claim credible Christian forgiveness.[21]

The five authors will all label as false a forgiveness that denies true feelings. A forgiveness which denies anger, jealousy, fear, resentment, etc., cannot be true forgiveness. Donnelly stresses the need for time in the forgiveness process. Forgiveness is false when one rushes past true feelings to a quick reconciliation which omits time for confrontation and dialogue.[22] The Linns agree with Donnelly's emphasis on timing in the reconciliation process[23] and caution that denying emotional woundedness can lead to adverse physical conditions.[24]

Patton claims that counseling clients to forgive as though forgiveness is an act or attitude is to proclaim salvation through good works.[25] A kind of forgiveness which fortifies itself with the defenses of rage, power, and righteousness cannot be true forgiveness.[26] Rather, true forgiveness "is not doing something but discovering something—that I am more like those who have hurt me than different from them."[27] Although true forgiveness "may involve confession of, and the sense of being forgiven for, specific sins, at its heart it is the recognition of my reception into the community of sinners—those affirmed by God as his children."[28]

Smedes suggests that forgiving is not forgetting, excusing, denying conflict, accepting another despite of shortcomings, or simply tolerating the other.[29] One must come to terms with the fact that anger and forgiveness live side by side in the same heart.[30]

The authors agree that true forgiveness is an important and necessary therapeutic goal. Augsburger understands forgiveness as a process that enables people to work through life's conflicts and enables those who forgive to restore alienated relationships. Forgiveness is important as a means of creating and recreating community.[31]

Donnelly suggests that the forgiving person looks beyond the sin of the other to focus on the other's worth as a person. Forgiveness is a power that counteracts negative energy generated by an offense. Forgiveness places the worth of the person above any accusation that might be leveled against that person.[32]

The Linns posit that the ability to forgive determines whether an emotional wound will evolve into a blessing or a curse. Forgiveness is a goal of a gradual process of healing that provides the blessing and energy needed to move into the future with hope.[33]

Patton takes seriously the difficulty many Christian clients have in forgiving those who are in close relationship with them.[34] Christian pastors' frequent inability to help clients find the path to forgiveness points not to the inappropriateness of forgiveness as a therapeutic goal, but to the inadequacy of the Christian concept of forgiveness.[35] Patton proposes that forgiveness be understood as a discovery of one's place within the sinful human community.[36] Forgiveness is not so much an active human process as it is part of a "larger process of reconciliation which is concretely expressed in human life through overcoming one's shame and rediscovering who one is beyond the experience of injury and brokenness."[37]

Smedes sees forgiveness as the only hope-filled and love-filled answer for an unfair world.[38] Forgiveness is a creative response to building a just world.[39]

While the pastoral authors contribute insights into the mystery of Christian forgiveness, one searches in vain for a uniform systematic theology of this forgiveness. Nevertheless, insights raised by the pastoral authors give clues suggesting elements essential to a contemporary understanding of Christian forgiveness; e.g., in order to respond to Augsburger a theology of forgiveness would need to wrestle with the possibility of communal reconciliation; in order to respond to Patton a contemporary understanding of forgiveness would need to describe the relationship between faith and works; in order to respond to the Linns a theology of forgiveness would need to include the possibility of experiential healing.

How Does the Christian Forgive?

The five authors agree that forgiveness is a process. Augsburger claims that the first step of the forgiveness process is to let go of the illusion of being innocent and to stand beside the offender in loving identification.[40] Valuing, loving the other, and canceling demands on him/her are essential to forgiveness.[41] Forgiveness involves truthful confrontation and demands repentance.[42] This repentance involves turning from mistrust of the other to trust, from safe withdrawal to risk, and also lovingly invites, through mutual dialogue, the other to change.[43] "When trust is restored and there is mutual recognition that constructive relationships have been resumed, forgiveness has become a reality."[44]

Donnelly asserts that the first step in the forgiveness process is to own the offense. The second step is to surrender this same offense to God. One must take responsibility for one's offense and then offer it to God who alone has the power to forgive, heal, and transform. Gratitude for the transforming power of God in one's own life enables one to be compassionate toward one's neighbor who is also a sinner.[45] The Christian thus imitates the forgiving Jesus who initiates the act of forgiveness, affirms self-worth, deals decisively with sin, cancels debts, and shifts the focus from self to God.[46]

The Linns apply Elizabeth Kübler-Ross's stages of death to the forgiveness process. According to this system, forgiveness has five stages: denial, anger, bargaining, depression, and acceptance.[47] Within each stage the Linns suggest the process of opening oneself to the unconditional love of God, of sharing one's feelings with Christ and listening to Christ's feelings, and finally of living out Christ's reaction.[48]

John Patton suggests that pastoral persons best serve their clients by providing an appropriate empathetic atmosphere that enables clients to shed the defenses that are blocking the discovery of forgiveness.[49] Understanding that one is part of the community of sinners unconditionally loved by God enables one to let go of rage, power, and righteousness. Forgiveness, according to Patton, is not so much an act; rather, one discovers the saving and reconciling power of Christ at work among those who are weak.[50]

Smedes outlines forgiveness as a four-stage process: hurt, hate, healing, and coming together.[51] Smedes suggests "redemptive remembering" as a healing way to deal with past hurts. In this type of remembering one does not forget or deny the past, but rather focuses one's energies on hopeful future possibilities.[52] Realizing that no human motivation is totally pure, forgiving accepts the reality of the human condition and forgives the offender out of the truthful acceptance that there is a mixture of good and evil in every human heart. Not to forgive one's neighbor, therefore, is to be out of touch with one's own reality.[53]

One can observe in these pastoral processes theological presuppositions concerning the tension between faith and works. Augsburger and Smedes stress forgiveness as an attitude or act. Their emphasis is on deciding to forgive and learning the interpersonal skills necessary to the process of forgiveness. Patton, on the other hand, emphasizes forgiveness as a discovery. The counselor, mirroring the unconditional regard and merciful love of God, facilitates an empathetic atmosphere wherein clients are free to gradually shed their defenses and discover themselves as part of the human community needing and experiencing the forgiving presence of God. In Patton's system the client's attempts to forgive or to be forgiving are seen as impediments to true forgiveness. Forgiveness is reduced to surrender and discovery. In Augsburger and Smedes one questions if persons trained in the skills of forgiveness might facilitate forgiveness adequately without the help of God. Forgiveness seems to be reduced to human decision, action, and skill.

In the course of her presentation, Donnelly outlines forgiveness as both action and surrender. Although the recognition of the tension between faith and works in the forgiveness process is suggested by Donnelly, development regarding the dynamics of this tension is cursory.

The Linns view the process of forgiveness primarily as a prayer dynamic. In each stage of the process one tells Christ how one feels, one listens to how Christ feels, and one then appropriates Christ's reaction. Forgiveness, although influenced by Christ, is largely controlled by the person forgiving. The emphasis is on the "work" of prayer in the forgiveness process. The Linns might have developed the tension between faith and works more successfully by following the lead of their mentor St. Ignatius of Loyola[54] in stressing the need to pray for particular graces needed in the spiritual journey.[55] This prayer for grace expresses both human action and also radical dependence upon the mercy and power of God.

What Is the Relationship Between
Forgiveness and Reconciliation?

The pastoral authors struggle with how the process of forgiveness effects reconciliation. For Augsburger, Christian forgiveness, especially with those with whom one is in relationship, requires genuine interpersonal reconciliation.[56] Since the community of persons is an image of the Trinitarian God,[57] a forgiveness which fails to build community cannot be authentic.[58]

Donnelly agrees that reconciliation must be the goal of forgiveness, but she stresses that this reconciliation must be prepared for and waited for.[59] Movements toward reconciliation are appropriate only when they respect the timing of the other and are motivated out of love for the other.[60]

The goal of the forgiving process for the Linns is the healing of painful memories. This healing allows the victim to understand the hurtful situation not as a curse but as a blessing.[61] One desires to see the situation with the eyes of Christ and strives to respond to the injury as Christ would respond. As one becomes aware of one's woundedness one also becomes aware of the woundedness of others. One joins a Christian community in order to minister together with others the healing power of Christ in a broken world.[62]

For Patton, one is able to forgive only after surrendering the power to forgive.[63] Reconciliation is possible when one discovers oneself united in "the community of sinners."[64] In the context of this community, one sees the neighbor as "a human being like oneself in spite of all that may have happened in that relationship."[65]

Although reconciliation of the parties involved is certainly the ideal, Smedes understands that there are times when this ideal cannot be realized. In this case one must do whatever is possible and be satisfied with even small success.[66] At times one must reduce expectations.[67] Because each person is a mixture of weakness and strength, one must leave room for the human element and realize that reconciliation will not always be perfect.[68]

The theological issues undergirding discussion of the relationship between forgiveness and reconciliation concern one's understanding of the dynamics between good and evil in light of the salvific action and victory of Christ. Christians believe that life has already conquered death, that good is victorious over evil, and yet they also bear the consequences of evil in their lives. How can one reconcile this apparent contradiction? If one forgives a neighbor who in turn refuses overtures of reconciliation, has not evil secured for itself victory through means of this division?

Augsburger insists that nothing less than Trinitarian communion is befitting a community claiming to be Christian. There are dangers in this position. Does such a community repress dissension and division in order to witness communion? Are prophetic personalities ostracized in order to protect a majority status quo?

Recognizing the need for time in the forgiveness process or realizing that the human community never experiences perfect reconciliation in its earthly journey are presuppositions that seem grounded in firmer experiential data. However, this common sense approach also presents theological difficulties. Christians are required to forgive but may or may not, either for appropriate reasons of their own or out of respect for the freedom of the other party, effect an interpersonal or communal reconciliation. In embracing such a theology does the Church undermine the salvific power of Christ? Does such an approach fail to keep alive a radical faith, hope, and love in both the neighbor and in God? If the truth which brings freedom to the human family can be found only in trinitarian communion, can a Christian Church conscientiously settle for anything less than reconciliation?

It was noted in the conclusion of Chapter 3 that a particular exegetical interpretation of the Lucan accounts of the prayer of forgiveness cannot be simplistically applied to pastoral situations of hurt and violence. Theological questions raised in pastoral practice continually challenge one's interpretation of the scriptural message. It is also obvious that pastoral theology is not unified in its concept of Christian forgiveness, in its process for approaching forgiveness as a counseling issue, or in its theology concerning the relationship between forgiveness and reconciliation. It is proposed that the dynamics of the Lucan prayer of forgiveness can serve as a systematic, organizing the insights of the five pastoral authors while respecting their unique contributions. This is the task of the final chapter.

Toward a Theology of Christian Forgiveness: A Scriptural/Pastoral Dialogue

The dialogue between the Lucan prayer of forgiveness and pastoral theologies of forgiveness evokes numerous theological insights concerning a contemporary understanding of the nature and process of Christian forgiveness. The goal of this chapter is to theologically reflect upon the Lucan prayer of forgiveness in light of the concerns of pastoral theology. This theological reflection will be systematized by returning to the three questions asked of the pastoral theologies in Chapter 4: (1) What is Christian forgiveness? (2) How does the Christian forgive? and (3) What is the relationship between forgiveness and reconciliation?

What Is Christian Forgiveness?

The stories of the prayer of forgiveness in the lives of Jesus and Stephen provide models of what forgiveness is and is not. One can observe in them that Christian forgiveness is a process centered in prayer and in eager expectation for the surprising action of God. One can see that both Jesus and Stephen suffer as they forgive. One understands that it is God who forgives and the human person who decides to invite the power of forgiveness into the realm of darkness and ignorance.

Lucan forgiveness involves human decision and action. The person decides to pray that God might forgive the enemy. This petitionary prayer is an essential element of the forgiveness process. People in Luke forgive by doing good to their oppressors, by returning a blessing for a curse, and by praying for those who mistreat them (Luke 6:27-28). When evil so binds their hands that they can no longer bless the one inflicting injury with acts of kindness, the Christian continues to bless the persecutor through prayer.

• Lucan forgiveness is an invitation to persecutors to repent of their ignorance. It is a refusal to exclude others from the reign of God by reason of the evil they have inflicted on an individual or on the Christian community. What is essential is that Christians neither give up on the persecutors, nor do they force their persecutors to obey the will of God as they understand it.

Lucan forgiveness is efficacious in accordance with the divine *dei*. The prayer of forgiveness invites God to break through the Babylon of sin and to establish the human community united in the Spirit of Jesus Christ. The divine *dei* is not conquered by ignorance, fear, or darkness. Rather God, if human persons ask, is able to use even darkness, fear, and ignorance for the good of the human community and for the glory and praise of God.

Forgiveness from the Lucan perspective is not devoid of justice. The Lucan corpus understands justice as a fruit of the coming of the reign of God. This justice rights even those wrongs occurring through acts of nature. In the day of the Lord the blind see and the deaf hear (Luke 4:18-19; 7:22). Luke understands the salvation brought about in Jesus not only in terms of the final eschaton, but also in terms of the eschatological kingdom breaking into human ignorance and darkness. The deed of justice is to invite the kingdom of God into these regions. Forgiveness is a deed of justice that believes and hopes in the other's salvation. In the prayer of forgiveness one continues to hold the other within the love of one's heart empowered with the Holy Spirit of God who alone has the power to love unconditionally.

The prayer of forgiveness becomes a means that Luke chooses to illustrate the role people play in their own salvation. To be saved one must repent (Acts 2:38), pray for those who hurt another (Luke 6:28), and listen to the Spirit of God (Luke 12:11-12).

Yet humans cannot save themselves. Once persons with a stance of repentance and openness to the Holy Spirit invite the power of God into the ignorance, fear, and darkness that bring conflict and confusion to the human family, then the power of God is able to unite and create community. This divine interaction is core to Luke's concept of forgiveness. It is powerfully evident in the Lucan corpus that even an integrated person such as Jesus or a strong leader such as Paul is unsuccessful in creating human community. Although human skills are helpful in the building of Christian community, Christian community is more than a mere product of human action; it is not even simply the product of human integration and holiness. Rather, Christian community is God's gift, given in response to human petition. While repentance and prayer ready the hearts of people to receive the gift of community, this human preparation must wait upon the mercy and the grace of God to bring it to fulfillment.

The Lucan corpus portrays forgiveness as a communal process. It involves the persecuted one, the persecutor, the entire human family, and the presence of the trinitarian God. Unilateral forgiveness is a non-entity in the Lucan tradition. Yet, in saying this, one does not mean that the persecuted ones and their persecutors will necessarily be at peace with each other even if those who perceive themselves as the persecuted come to a degree of peace through the prayer of forgiveness.

Disciples always hope for the repentance of their persecutors and, because they share in the same unconditional love of God as does the persecutor, are able to hold their arms wide in a desire to be in communion with their persecutors. However, the paths of repentance and peace for the persecutors may take a very different form than the paths of repentance and peace experienced by the victims. At times, especially when there has been no previous relationship with the offenders, it is sufficient to pray and to hope for their salvation while allowing them the freedom to follow and choose their own path. The grace of Pentecost is given to the repentant. It is not forced on anyone.

Thus while forgiveness is essentially communal, it does not guarantee a fused vision. The trinitarian image of community with room for personalities within a union of love is helpful here. The persecutor and the persecuted may, even after much prayer and work, not understand life in the same way. What is essential is that they appreciate each other's place within the trinitarian union of love. Since God excludes no one, persons who try to cut off a brother or sister from the reign of God only succeed in isolating themselves. The reconciliation of God allows those with differing gifts and worldviews to be united in love without demanding that they strip themselves of personality for the sake of fusion. While adherence to a dominating ideology brings sterility and rebellion, trinitarian communion fosters the actualization of individual personalities and gifts for the good of the community and the glory of God.

Although the pastoral theologians studied do not develop the concept of Christian forgiveness in the same way Luke does, there are a number of common themes. David Augsburger proposes that forgiveness is that quality which enables people to work through the tensions and conflicts of life in order to persevere in relationship to each other.[1] Luke certainly agrees that forgiveness is a bond of Christian community. However, there is a strong emphasis in Luke that this bonding is both a work and a grace. While one works toward the realization of forgiveness, one also prays for the grace of forgiveness.

Doris Donnelly suggests that forgiveness looks beyond the sin of the other and focuses on the other's worth as a person.[2] Luke agrees that it is the love of the other that is primary. This love is rooted in truth. Forgiveness is a work and a grace of truth that is accomplished in and through the love of God and neighbor. The deed and grace of forgiveness is most effectively accomplished when Christians do the works of justice and continue to love and pray in the midst of confusion and hurt.

Dennis and Matthew Linn understand that a sign that healing has occurred through the forgiveness process is gratitude for past hurts. One is grateful because one sees these past hurts as a reason for growth.[3] This healing, according to Luke, occurs in and for the community. It is a healing that enables the reign of God to manifest itself within the human community. One is healed for the mission of the Church.

John Patton finds it difficult to understand forgiveness in terms of human attitude or action alone.[4] For him, pastoral practice confirms that many Christian clients find it difficult to forgive.[5] While Patton prefers to stress forgiveness as a discovery of the grace of God already operative,[6] Luke understands the dynamic of forgiveness to include a human response that not only discovers but also invites. For Luke, forgiveness is already present in the unconditional love of God for all; it is made operative through human invitation; and it creates Christian community through the surprising action of God.

Lewis Smedes understands forgiveness as a creative response to building a new beginning out of pain that never should have existed.[7] While it is true that forgiveness is creative and, as Doris Donnelly suggests, often needs to be carefully and imaginatively planned within the context of love for the other,[8] it is more than mere creative human action. Forgiveness as the only hope-filled and love-filled answer for an unfair world[9] depends upon the interrelationship between human action and divine love.

In summary, the pastoral theologians struggle to articulate the concept of forgiveness as the reality of the love of God faithfully present within the human community, as a human action, and as a divine force which creatively brings about reconciliation. Luke successfully weaves all three elements within the dynamics of the prayer of forgiveness. Forgiveness happens within the context of the unconditional love of God. It is activated through human invitation, deeds of justice, and repentance, and it is made effective through the reconciling power and grace of the Holy Spirit.

How Does the Christian Forgive?

The three dynamics of the prayer of forgiveness offer theological insights into the Christian process of forgiveness. These dynamics—the prayer asking God to forgive the enemy, the prayer of surrender, and expectant waiting for the manifestation of the power of God-provide a framework within which the theologian might suggest insights to guide pastoral counselors in their facilitation of the forgiveness process within the lives of individual clients.

The salvific power of the forgiveness of God in the Lucan corpus is given to those with repentant hearts. After Jesus prays the prayer of forgiveness, the Good Thief repents of his sin and is promised salvation "today" (Luke 23:40-43). The people who beat their breasts after the crucifixion of Jesus (Luke 23:48) return on Pentecost and are baptized (Acts 2:37-41). On the road toward Emmaus, Jesus challenges the disciples' assessment of the situation requiring forgiveness (Luke 24:13-35). Openness to this challenge is, according to Luke, a prerequisite to the process of forgiveness.

The prayer of forgiveness invites a posture of repentance. Tendencies towards labeling and blaming become softened in prayer. Judgments that initially seem polarized become more nuanced. Through the prayer of forgiveness, one eventually recognizes oneself among the "they" who "know not what they are doing" (Luke 23:34).

This deepening sense of social consciousness and unity with all human persons may initially bring pain and confusion. Although it does not seem fair that one be united to the guilt of the world it becomes understandable that one indeed cannot be separated from the unfortunate circumstances of another. The situation of evil teaches that violence against one person can easily be redirected toward another who might be quite unsuspecting. What at first seems a cut and dried case of victimization may through insight and prayer be perceived as tainted with one's own guilt. The client, as John Patton proposes, becomes aware that sin is not the property of a single individual or a particular group.[10] To sentence the other to the full burden of blame becomes less and less acceptable.

The Lucan corpus portrays even the most integrated of persons as powerless to bring about reconciliation. This realization of powerlessness is particularly heightened if one has exhausted oneself attempting to bring about the desired reconciliation. It is even more evident if the persecutor has cut off options in such a way that one is no longer able to perform acts of kindness for the persecutor. At this juncture it seems that the possibility for reconciliation is aborted. All appearances suggest that evil has conquered good. The sky is darkened (Luke 23:44) and the people beat their breasts and go home (Luke 23:48).

When these movements are recognized, the Lucan dynamic suggests the prayer of surrender. In this prayer disciples surrender their future and mission to the mercy and power of God. Disciples hand everything over to God who they understand as the only one capable of effecting reconciliation. Luke proposes that disciples who do their best to follow the will of God will indeed experience persecution, but, if they persevere in faith, hope, and love will, through this very persecution, fulfill their mission and purpose in life (Luke 9:23-24). Disciples who follow Jesus and Stephen in offering the prayer of surrender will have the restraints holding their mission in bondage broken through the reconciling power of the Holy Spirit.

While grace builds on nature—interpersonal skills and techniques are essential and necessary for fostering Christian community—nature cannot bring about its own salvation. Forgiveness is a salvific divine and human interaction that requires more than interpersonal skills. Grace without human invitation will wait for such an invitation. Human invitation awaiting the moment of grace must allow itself to be purified in surrender.

Finally, the process of Lucan forgiveness offers theological insights into the mystery of reconciliation as a grace. The prayer of forgiveness in the Lucan corpus is in both cases almost immediately efficacious. However, this efficaciousness is apparent only to those who have eyes to see the working of the grace of God. By focusing on the manifestations of God's grace rather than solely on their injuries, disciples are able to see and respond to the salvation and forgiveness they desire. In the Lucan corpus those who receive the grace of forgiveness are sent to share and proclaim this grace to others (Luke 24:47).

The five pastoral theologians stress forgiveness as a process and develop one or more of the dynamics found in the Lucan literature. David Augsburger understands forgiveness as the means to creative community.[11] His insistence that one must let go of the illusions of innocence and stand beside the offender in loving identification is certainly in line with Luke's message.[12] Augsburger suggests that one must trust and risk until authentic reconciliation is perceived by both parties.[13] This movement toward reconciliation involves accepting the past and actively choosing one's future behavior.[14] Community is the product of such trust, risk, and repentance.[15]

Although the risen Jesus in Luke does appear to the disciples, bringing them peace and hope, it is not these deeds of reconciliation and justice alone that bring forth Christian community. The Lucan Jesus tells his disciples to wait for the coming of the Holy Spirit (Luke 24:49; Acts 1:4-5). Thus without denying David Augsburger's stress on human responsibility and action, Luke proposes that more than human responsibility and action are necessary. Christian community also requires that the bond of the Holy Spirit be given to those who pray and repent. The grace of reconciliation can be invited by humans, but it cannot be controlled.

Doris Donnelly stresses the necessity of first owning the offense and then surrendering the offense to God who has the power to heal and transform.[16] Dennis and Matthew Linn understand the need to appropriate the vision of Christ.[17] In these authors one can see that there is a dynamic of the forgiveness process that extends beyond the realm of human action. Luke proclaims and celebrates this dynamic as the Spirit of God who breaks into the moment of hurt and violence. For Luke, the salvation of the individual is always within the context of and to the betterment of the community.

John Patton points to the unconditional love of God as the foundation of all forgiveness. Forgiveness occurs when one discovers oneself within a community of sinners who are loved and saved by the unconditional mercy of God.[18] While Patton's stress on grace in the forgiveness process is a refreshing one, his concept of the forgiveness process is different from Luke's. Without denying Patton's contribution, Luke demands repentance, deeds of justice, and prayer. These human actions are indeed central to forgiveness. It is through the invitation of human petition and action that the forgiveness of God, already present, is invited into the human sphere. Persons are called to discover forgiveness, pray for forgiveness, act through forgiveness, and celebrate the glory of God present in the forgiveness that bonds them together into community and in praise of God.

Lewis Smedes outlines the process of forgiveness in four stages: hurt, hate, healing, and coming together.[19] Hate can take both passive and aggressive forms. Passive hate is the unwillingness to bless another or to wish the other well. Aggressive hate is a fury that wishes another ill. Hate usually occurs between people who are in close relationship; anger occurs between strangers.[20]

Luke does portray Jesus as angry (Luke 19:45-46) but not as hateful. In fact it is precisely because Jesus does not hate that his passion is salvific. Like Stephen, faithful Christian disciples are challenged to persevere in faith, hope, and love until the end.

One sees that each of the pastoral authors contributes insight into one or more of the Lucan dynamics. The Lucan prayer of forgiveness offers a paradigm by which the theologian might be challenged to discern further the relationship between grace and human action in the forgiveness process.

Lucan forgiveness is a process. It is accomplished within the context of the unconditional love and mercy of God, the call this love and mercy demand of persons to perform deeds of justice, as well as the call to repentance. It involves praying that God might forgive the enemy, surrendering one's life and mission into the hands of God who alone has the power to bring true reconciliation, and waiting expectantly for the power of God to create a new and vibrant community from people torn apart by hurt and violence.

What Is the Relationship Between Forgiveness and Reconciliation?

The theologian using the Lucan paradigm could insist that forgiveness must involve reconciliation and also that it does not necessarily involve reconciliation. One could take one or the other position depending on one's concept of reconciliation. The Lucan evidence does not present the prayer of forgiveness in the lives of Jesus and Stephen as effective in bringing about a common and peaceful solution to an immediate crisis. Both Jesus and Stephen lived lives and spoke prophetic words that angered those who preferred the status quo to repentance. The reality is that both Jesus and Stephen are killed. Their death scenes offer no apparent evidence of reconciliation with their persecutors.

On the other hand, the stories of Jesus and Stephen demonstrate that reconciliation is central to the forgiveness process. Neither Jesus nor Stephen close off the possibility of a change of heart in their persecutors. Their prayer of forgiveness offers no judgment which attempts to exclude the other from the reign of God. While their prayer welcomes the other into trinitarian community, it does not dictate the form of this community. The form reconciliation takes is dependent upon the creative action of God.

Reconciliation is seen by Luke not merely as the mission of the disciple, but also as God's choice to enter human confusion and violence. Reconciliation occurs because God is invited and is eager to respond. However, God who knows each one's heart responds in a way that creates reconciliation yet unheard of by either party. In observing what the power of God will do in the act of reconciliation, it may be necessary to die to preconceived notions of reconciliation in order that God might be free to resurrect one's hopes and dreams in a new form.

Luke would agree with David Augsburger's tenet that genuine forgiveness does demand reconciliation.[21] However, Luke suggests that this reconciliation is the surprise of God in accordance with the divine *dei* and is effective in creative ways. The will of the other is always respected in the Lucan literature. The forgiveness of God, while offered to all, is effective among those who repent, do the deeds of justice, and pray. The power of God, operative through the love of community members, witnesses the advantage of conversion to those with hardened hearts. Even when evil seems to have conquered good, the Lucan vision understands that God is always the victor, and will, if God is invited into the darkness through the persevering prayer of a Christian, create Christian community out of the chaos and darkness.

Dennis and Matthew Linn understand the goal of forgiveness to be the healing of painful memories that allows the victim to understand a situation of evil as a blessing rather than as a curse.[22] This inner reconciliation is possible because one is able to see life with the vision of Christ. Luke offers the disciples going to Emmaus this same opportunity. In helping these disciples appropriate the message of the Scriptures to their particular dilemma, Jesus brings hope and reconciliation.

John Patton perceives forgiveness as the discovery that one is more like those who have injured than unlike them.[23] Luke recognizes the need for repentance in order for grace to be effective. Luke would agree with Patton that the unconditional love of God for persons united in sin is the foundation of forgiveness. While one discovers forgiveness within the context of unconditional love, one also needs to explore as central to forgiveness the purpose of human activity, the surrendering of one's life and mission into the hands of God, and experience of the grace of the Holy Spirit which forms community.

Lewis Smedes posits that the goal of forgiveness is not to deny the past, but rather to remember the past in order to own it and be challenged by the opportunities it offers. In this "redemptive remembering" one focuses one's energies on hopeful future possibilities.[24] Luke agrees with this insight but grounds it in the prayers of forgiveness and surrender. One expects the power of the Holy Spirit at its appointed time to break into a chaotic situation only after the human community has united itself in repentance and prayer.

In summary, Luke offers a concept of reconciliation within the context of the forgiveness process which includes insights from pastoral theology and expands upon them. For Luke, reconciliation is essential to the forgiveness process, but this reconciliation is accomplished according to the divine *dei* and not according to human design. Reconciliation is offered to all but can be accepted only by those whose hearts are prepared for it. The prayer of forgiveness challenges attitudes of labeling and blaming; it encourages the Christian community to continue to invite those who inflict injury on the community or on its individual members. It is through doing good to and praying for the persecutor that the grace of God is given and the Pentecostal miracle of love continues to deepen and grow.

Conclusion

The contribution of the Lucan prayer of forgiveness is its presentation of Christian forgiveness as both a human and divine interaction and its illustration of the dynamics of this interaction. Forgiveness is an expression of the unconditional love of God, activated by human invitation, repentance, and deeds of justice, that invites the Spirit of God to creatively build Christian community out of darkness and chaos. It is a process that draws human community into the very dynamics of trinitarian life. This inclusion within the reign of God already present enables Christians with the persistence of God to love those who hate them. The prayer of forgiveness is a sign of this persistence and an efficacious assurance that love is indeed the victor.

It is evident from the preceding dialogue that pastoral theology has done much to clarify a pastoral theory of Christian forgiveness. Using the three dynamics of the Lucan prayer of forgiveness: (1) the choice to pray that God might forgive the enemy, (2) the surrendering of one's spirit to God, and (3) the manifestation of God's fidelity, as one possible paradigm, it has been demonstrated that the five pastoral theologies studied contribute insight and contemporary development to the Lucan perspective. While each author speaks in some respect to the Lucan dynamics, no author explores them completely.

The Lucan prayer of forgiveness weaves key theological concerns, e.g., the relationship between faith and works in the forgiveness process, the struggle to understand the relationship between justice and forgiveness, the process of forgiveness, and the relationship between forgiveness and reconciliation, into its dynamics. By using the Lucan prayer of forgiveness as a theological paradigm, a theologian can evaluate and situate the contributions of pastoral authors. Critical dialogue between the Lucan prayer of forgiveness and pastoral theologies of forgiveness is valuable in that it grounds theological theories of forgiveness in experience, and offers pastoral practice a deepening theological foundation.

The insights rising from this critical dialogue between the dynamics of the Lucan prayer of forgiveness and selected pastoral theologies invite further investigation. Systematic theologians might appropriate the above findings to their discussions of Christology, soteriology, ecclesiology, eschatology, etc. For example, the Lucan contribution has the potential to guide soteriologists in their struggle to articulate human and divine interaction operative in the Christian experience of salvation.

Some ramifications of the Lucan prayer of forgiveness to ecclesiology have already been suggested. The ecclesiologist, however, would be interested in a more complete development. An interesting hypothesis would be to explore the existence and formation of new forms of Christian communities that have arisen from the prayer of forgiveness uttered during times of persecution and violence.

An eschatologist might find the prayer of forgiveness helpful in the struggle to articulate the present and future reality of the reign of God. The Lucan contribution provides a paradigm by which the theologian could study realistic expectations of the coming of the reign of God into the human community. One might also examine the freedom and joy experienced by those suffering the pain of persecution and yet grounded, as Stephen was, in the eschatological vision.

Moral theologians could explore implications of the Lucan prayer of forgiveness in their concerns regarding war and peace, divorce and remarriage, pacifism and non-violence, etc. The Lucan prayer of forgiveness respects the freedom of another, while continuing to invite the other into relationship. How one continues to invite another, whose heart is hardened, into relationship poses complex moral questions.

Finally, pastoral theologians might develop the insights obtained from this dialogue into a systematic pastoral theory of forgiveness. This theory might include the three Lucan dynamics and the contributions of pastoral and psychological theorists who have already explored one or more aspects of the Lucan prayer of forgiveness.

Bibliography

Reference Works

Aland, Kurt. *Synopsis of the Four Gospels: Greek-English Edition of the Synopsis Quattuor Evangeliorum.* Stuttgart: German Bible Society, 1984.

_____. *Vollständige Konkordanz zum griechischen Neuen Testament unter Zugrundelegung aller modernen kritischen Textausgaben und des Textus receptus.* Berlin: Walter de Gruyter, 1983.

Black, Matthew, and H. H. Rowley, eds. *Peake's Commentary on the Bible.* London: Thomas Nelson and Sons Ltd., 1963. S.v. "Luke," by G.W.H. Lampe.

Brown, Raymond E., and others, eds. *The New Jerome Biblical Commentary.* Englewood Cliffs, N.J.: Prentice Hall, 1990. S.v. "The Gospel According to Luke" by Robert J. Karris.

Bruce, Alexander B. *See* Nicoll, W. Robertson, ed. 1912.

Bultmann, Rudolf. *See* Kittel, Gerhard, ed. 1964.

Buttrick, George A. and others, eds. *The Interpreter's Bible.* Vol. 8, *The Gospel According to St. Luke.* Exposition on chs. 19–24 by Paul Scherer. New York: Abingdon Press, 1952.

Hastings, James, and others, eds. *A Dictionary of Christ and the Gospels.* New York: Charles Scribner's Sons, 1908. S.v. "Prayer" by A. Plummer.

Karris, Robert J. *See* Brown, Raymond E., and others, eds., 1990.

Kittel, Gerhard. *Theological Dictionary of the New Testament*, vol. 1, Geoffrey W. Bromiley, ed. and trans. Grand Rapids, Mich.: Wm. B. Eerdmans Publishing Company, 1964. S.v. *Agōnia* by Ethelbert Stauffer and *Aphiemi* by Rudolf Bultmann.

Lampe, G.W.H. *See* Black, Matthew, and H. H. Rowley, eds. 1963.

Metzger, Bruce M. *A Textual Commentary on the Greek New Testament.* London: United Bible Societies, 1971.

Nestle, E. and K. Aland, eds. *Novum Testamentum Graece.* 26th ed. Stuttgart: Deutsche Bibelgesellschaft, 1979.

Nicoll, W. Robertson, ed. *The Expositor's Greek Testament.* Vol. 1, pt. 1, *The Synoptic Gospels* by Alexander B. Bruce. London: Hodder and Stoughton, 1912.

Plummer, A. *See* Hastings, James, and others, eds. 1908.

Scherer, Paul. *See* Buttrick, George A., and others, eds. 1952.

Stauffer, Ethelbert. *See* Kittel, Gerhard, ed. 1964.

Strack, Hermann L., and Paul Billerbeck. *Kommentarzum Neuen Testament aus Talmud und Midrasch.* Vol. 2. München: C. H. Becksche Verlagsbuchhandlung Oskar Beck, 1924.

Westcott, Brooke, and Fenton Hort. *The New Testament in the Original Greek.* Vol. 2. Introduction and Appendix. New York: Harper and Brothers, 1882.

Other Literature

Al-Mabuk, Radhi Hasan. "The Commitment to Forgive in Parentally Love-Deprived College Students." Ph.D. diss., University of Wisconsin-Madison, 1990.

Augsburger, David. *Caring Enough To Forgive: True Forgiveness* and *Caring Enough To Not Forgive: False Forgiveness.* Ventura, Calif.: Regal Books, 1981.

_____. *Helping People Forgive.* Louisville: Westminster John Knox Press, 1996.

Bailie, Gil. *Violence Unveiled: Humanity at the Crossroads.* New York: Crossroad, 1995.

Barnes, T. D. "Legislation Against the Christians." *Journal of Roman Studies* 58 (1968) 32–50.

Bauer, Yehuda, Alice Eckhard and Franklin Littell, eds. *Remembering for the Future.* Vol. 1, *Jews and Christians During and After the Holocaust.* New York: Pergamon Press, 1989.

Beck, Brian E. "*Imitatio Christi* and the Lucan Passion Narrative." In *Suffering and Martyrdom in the New Testament,* William Horbury and Brian McNeil, eds., 28–47. Cambridge: Cambridge University Press, 1981.

Bock, Darrell L. *Proclamation From Prophecy and Pattern: Lucan Old Testament Christology.* Journal for the Study of the New Testament Supplement Series 12. Sheffield, England: Sheffield Academic Press, 1987.

Boff, Leonardo. *O destino do homen e do mundo: Ensaio sobre a vocação humana.* Petrópolis: Editora Vozes Ltda., 1973.

Boman, T. "Das letzte Wort Jesu." *Studia theologica* 17 (1963) 103–19.

Brandsma, Jeffrey M. "Forgiveness: A Dynamic, Theological and Therapeutic Analysis." *Pastoral Psychology* 31:1 (1982) 40–50.

Brink, T. L. "The Role of Religion in Later Life: A Case of Consolation and Forgiveness." *Journal of Psychology and Christianity* 4:2 (1985) 22–5.

Brown, Raymond. "The Pater Noster as an Eschatological Prayer." *Theological Studies* 22:2 (1961) 175–208.

Brown, Schuyler. *Apostasy and Perseverance in the Theology of Luke.* Rome: Pontifical Biblical Institute, 1969.

Buckley, Thomas W. *Seventy Times Seven: Sin, Judgment, and Forgiveness in Matthew.* Zacchaeus Studies: New Testament Series. Collegeville: The Liturgical Press, 1991.

Carroll, John T. *Response to the End of History: Eschatology and Situation in Luke-Acts.* SBL Dissertation Series, 92. Atlanta, Ga.: Scholars Press, 1988.

Cassidy, Richard J. *Jesus, Politics, and Society: A Study of Luke's Gospel.* Maryknoll, N.Y.: Orbis Books, 1978.

_____. *Society and Politics in the Acts of the Apostles.* Maryknoll, N.Y.: Orbis Books, 1987.

Cone, James. *God of the Oppressed.* New York: The Seabury Press, 1975.

Conn, Harvie M. "Luke's Theology of Prayer." *Christianity Today* 17:6 (1972) 290–2.

Conzelmann, Hans. *The Theology of St. Luke.* Geoffrey Buswell, trans. New York: Harper and Row Publishers, 1960.

Cosgrove, Charles H. "The Divine *dei* in Luke-Acts: Investigations into the Lukan Understanding of God's Providence." *Novum Testamentum* 26:2 (1984) 168–90.

Creed, John M. *The Gospel According to St. Luke*. London: Macmillan, 1930.

Crowe, Jerome. "The Laos at the Cross: Luke's Crucifixion Scene." In *The Language of the Cross,* Aelred Lacomara, ed., 75–101. Chicago: Franciscan Herald Press, 1977.

Crump, David Michael. "Jesus the Intercessor: Prayer and Christology in Luke-Acts." Ph.D. diss., University of Aberdeen (United Kingdom) 1988.

Curtis, Nathaniel C. "The Structure and Dynamics of Forgiving Another." Ph.D. diss., United States International University, 1989.

Dalman, Gustaf. *Jesus-Jeshua: Studies in the Gospels*. Translated by Paul P. Levertoff. London: S.P.C.K., 1929; reprint, New York: KTAV Publishing House, Inc., 1971.

Daly, Mary. "After the Death of God the Father: Women's Liberation and the Transformation of Christian Consciousness." In *Womanspirit Rising: A Feminist Reader in Religion*. Carol P. Christ and Judith Plaskow, eds., 53–67. San Francisco: Harper and Row Publishers, 1979.

Danker, Frederick W. *Jesus and the New Age According to St. Luke: A Commentary on the Third Gospel*. St. Louis, Mo.: Clayton Publishing House, 1972.

_____. *Jesus and the New Age: A Commentary on St. Luke's Gospel*. Philadelphia: Fortress Press, 1988.

Darrett, Susan R. *The Demise of the Devil: Magic and the Demonic in Luke's Writings*. Minneapolis: Fortress Press, 1989.

Daube, D. "For They Know Not What They Do: Luke 23,34." *Studia Patristica* IV (1961) 58–70.

Dawsey, James M. *The Lucan Voice: Confusion and Irony in the Gospel of Luke*. Macon, Ga.: Mercer University, 1986.

Dibelius, Martin. *From Tradition to Gospel*. Translated from the revised second edition by Bertram Lee Woolf. Greenwood, S.C.: The Attic Press, Inc., 1971.

Donnelly, Doris. "Forgiveness and Recidivism." *Pastoral Psychology* 33:1 (1984) 15–24.

_____. *Learning To Forgive*. Nashville, Tenn.: Abingdon Press, 1979.

_____. *Putting Forgiveness Into Practice*. Allen, Tex.: Argus Communications, 1982.

Downie, R. S. "Forgiveness." *Philosophical Quarterly* 15:59 (1965) 128–34.

Droll, David Michael. "Forgiveness: Theory and Research." Ph.D. diss., University of Nevada, 1984.

Dupont, Jacques. "Conversion in the Acts of the Apostles." In *The Salvation of the Gentiles: Studies in the Acts of the Apostles*. John R. Keating, trans. New York: Paulist Press, 1979.

Duquoc, Christian. "The Forgiveness of God." Translated by Iain McGonagle. In *Forgiveness*, Casiano Floristán and Christian Duquoc, eds., 35–44. Concilium Religion in the Eighties Series, 184:2. Edinburgh: T. & T. Clark Ltd., 1986.

Eastin, David L. "The Treatment of Adult Female Incest Survivors by Psychological Forgiveness Processes." Ph.D. diss., The University of Wisconsin-Madison, 1989.

Ellis, E. Earle. *The Gospel of Luke*. Greenwood, S.C.: The Attic Press, Inc., 1974.

Enright, Robert D., Maria J. Santos and Radhi Al-Mabuk. "The Adolescent as Forgiver." *Journal of Adolescence* 12:1 (1989) 95–110.

Enright, Robert D., and Robert L. Zell. "Problems Encountered When We Forgive One Another." *Journal of Psychology and Christianity* 8:1 (1989) 52–60.

Eusebius of Caesarea. *Historia ecclesiastica*. In *Die griechischen christlichen Schriftsteller der ersten drei Jahrhunderte*, vol. 9:1–3. E. Schwartz, ed. Berlin: J. C. Hinrichs (1903, 1908).

Fascher, Erich. "Theologische Beobachtungen zu *dei*." In *Neutestamentliche Studien für Rudolf Bultmann*, W. Eltester, ed., 228–54. Berlin: Alfred Töpelmann, 1954.

Fichtner, Joseph A. "Christ Humiliated and Exalted." *Worship* 36:5 (1962) 308–13.

Fiorenza, Elisabeth Schüssler. "The Ethics of Biblical Interpretation: Decentering Biblical Scholarship." *Journal of Biblical Literature* 107 (1988) 3–17.

Fitzgibbons, Richard P. "The Cognitive and Emotive Uses of Forgiveness in the Treatment of Anger." *Psychotherapy* 23:4 (1986) 629–33.

Fitzmyer, Joseph A. *The Gospel According to Luke I-IX.* Anchor Bible 28. Garden City, N.Y.: Doubleday and Company, Inc., 1981.

_____. *The Gospel According to Luke X-XXIV.* Anchor Bible 28A. Garden City, N.Y.: Doubleday and Company, Inc., 1985.

_____. *Luke the Theologian: Aspects of His Teaching.* New York: Paulist Press, 1989.

Flanigan, Beverly J. "Shame and Forgiving in Alcoholism." *Alcoholism Treatment Quarterly* 4:2 (1987) 181–95.

Ford, J. Massyngbaerde. *My Enemy Is My Guest: Jesus and Violence in Luke.* Maryknoll, N.Y.: Orbis Books, 1984.

_____. "Reconciliation and Forgiveness in Luke's Gospel." In *Political Issues in Luke-Acts,* Richard J. Cassidy and Philip J. Scharper, eds., 80–98. Maryknoll, N.Y.: Orbis Books, 1983.

Fow, Neil Robert. "The Empirical Phenomenological Investigation of the Experience of Forgiving Another." Ph.D. diss., University of Pittsburgh, 1988.

Franklin, Eric. *Christ the Lord: A Study in the Purpose and Theology of Luke-Acts.* Philadelphia: The Westminster Press, 1975.

Frend, W.H.C. *Martyrdom and Persecution in the Early Church: A Study of a Conflict from the Maccabees to Donatus.* Garden City, N.Y.: Doubleday and Company, Inc., 1967.

Gartner, John. "The Capacity to Forgive: An Object Relations Perspective." *Journal of Religion and Health* 27:4 (1988) 313–20.

Girard, René. *The Scapegoat.* Translated by Yvonne Freccero. Baltimore: The Johns Hopkins University Press, 1986.

Green, Joel B. "The Death of Jesus, God's Servant." In *Reimaging the Death of the Lukan Jesus,* Dennis D. Sylva, ed., 1–28. Athenäums Monografien, Bonner Biblische Beiträge 73 Frankfurt: Hain, 1990.

Häring, Bernard. *Free and Faithful in Christ: Moral Theology for Priests and Laity*. Vol. 2, *The Truth Will Set You Free*. New York: The Seabury Press, 1979.

Harris, Lindell O. "Prayer in the Gospel of Luke." *Southwestern Journal of Theology* 10:1 (1967) 59–69.

Harris, Oscar Gerald. "Prayer in Luke-Acts: A Study in the Theology of Luke." Ph.D. diss., Vanderbilt University, 1966.

Hebl, John Howard. "Forgiveness as a Counseling Goal with Elderly Females." Ph.D. diss., University of Wisconsin-Madison, 1990.

Hezel, Francis X. "'Conversion' and 'Repentance' in Lucan Theology." *The Bible Today* 37 (1968) 2596–602.

Hope, Donald. "The Healing Paradox of Forgiveness." *Psychotherapy* 24:2 (1987) 240–4.

Hultgren, Arland J. "Paul's Prechristian Persecutions of the Church: Their Purpose, Locale and Nature." *Journal of Biblical Literature* 95:1 (1976) 97–111.

Ignatius of Antioch. "Epistula ad Ephesios." In *Die apostolischen Väter*, Funk and Bihlmeyer, eds., 82–8. 2nd ed. Tübingen: J.C.B. Mohr, 1956.

Ignatius of Loyola. *The Spiritual Exercises: A Literal Translation and A Contemporary Reading*. David L. Fleming, S.J., ed. St. Louis: The Institute of Jesuit Sources, 1978.

Irenaeus of Lyons. *Adversus haereses*. W. W. Harvey, ed. Cambridge: Cambridge University Press, 1857.

Jeremias, Joachim. *The Prayers of Jesus*. John Bowden, Christoph Burchard, and John Reumann, trans. Studies in Biblical Theology, 2nd Series 6. Naperville, Ill.: Alec R. Allenson, Inc., 1967.

Jones, Gregory L. *Embodying Forgiveness: A Theological Analysis*. Grand Rapids, Mich.: William B. Eerdmans Publishing Company, 1995.

Juel, Donald. *Luke-Acts: The Promise of History*. Atlanta, Ga.: John Knox Press, 1983.

Karris, Robert J. *Luke: Artist and Theologian: Luke's Passion Account as Literature*. New York: Paulist Press, 1985.

_____. "Luke 23:47 and the Lucan View of Jesus' Death." *Journal of Biblical Literature* 105:1 (1986) 65–74.

_____. "Missionary Communities: A New Paradigm for the Study of Luke-Acts." *Catholic Biblical Quarterly* 41:1 (1979) 80–97.

_____. *What Are They Saying about Luke and Acts?: A Theology of the Faithful God.* New York: Paulist Press, 1979.

Kodell, Jerome. "Luke's Theology of the Death of Jesus." In *Sin, Salvation, and the Spirit,* Daniel Durken, ed., 221–30. Collegeville: The Liturgical Press, 1979.

Kübler-Ross, Elizabeth. *On Death and Dying.* New York: The Macmillan Company, 1969.

Lampe, G.W.H. "'Grievous Wolves' (Acts 20:29)." In *Christ and Spirit in the New Testament,* Barnabas Lindars and Stephen Smalley, eds., 253–68. Cambridge: Cambridge University Press, 1973.

_____. *God As Spirit: The Bampton Lectures, 1976.* Oxford: Clarendon Press, 1977.

_____. "Martyrdom and Inspiration." In *Suffering and Martyrdom in the New Testament,* William Horbury and Brian McNeil, eds., 118–35. Cambridge: Cambridge University Press, 1981.

_____. "The Holy Spirit in the Writings of St. Luke." In *Studies in the Gospels: Essays in Memory of R. H. Lightfoot,* D. E. Nineham, ed., 159–200. Oxford: Basil Blackwell, 1967.

LaVerdiere, Eugene. *Luke.* Wilmington, Del.: Michael Glazier, Inc., 1980.

Léon-Dufour, Xavier. *Life and Death in the New Testament: The Teachings of Jesus and Paul.* Terrence Prendergast, trans. San Francisco: Harper and Row Publishers, 1986.

Linn, Dennis, and Matthew Linn. *Healing Life's Hurts: Healing Memories Through Five Stages of Forgiveness.* New York: Paulist Press, 1978.

Lohse, Eduard. *The New Testament Environment.* John E. Steely, trans. Nashville, Tenn.: Abingdon, 1976.

Maddox, Robert. *The Purpose of Luke-Acts.* Edinburgh: T. & T. Clark, 1982.

Marshall, I. Howard. *The Gospel of Luke: A Commentary on the Greek Text*. Grand Rapids, Mich.: William B. Eerdmans Publishing Company, 1978.

_____. *Luke: Historian and Theologian*. Grand Rapids, Mich.: Zondervan Publishing House, 1970.

Martin, Ralph P. "Salvation and Discipleship in Luke's Gospel." *Interpretation* 30:4 (1976) 366–80.

Matera, Frank. "The Death of Jesus According to Luke: A Question of Sources." *Catholic Biblical Quarterly* 47 (1985) 469–85.

_____. "Luke 22, 66-71: Jesus Before the Presbyterion." *Ephemerides Theologicae Lovaniensis* 65:1 (1989) 43–59.

_____. *Passion Narratives and Gospel Theologies: Interpreting the Synoptics Through Their Passion Stories*. New York: Paulist Press, 1986.

Merkel, Helmut. "The Opposition Between Jesus and Judaism." In *Jesus and the Politics of His Day*, Ernst Bammel and C.F.D. Moule, eds., 129–44. Cambridge: Cambridge University Press, 1984.

Minear, Paul S. "A Note on Luke xxii 36." *Novum Testamentum* 7 (1964) 128–34.

Moltmann, Jürgen. *The Crucified God: The Cross of Christ as the Foundation and Criticism of Christian Theology*. R. A. Wilson and John Bowden, trans. New York: Harper & Row, 1974.

Moule, C.F.D. *Essays in New Testament Interpretation*. Cambridge: Cambridge University Press, 1982.

Mueller, Joan. *Why Can't I Forgive You?: A Christian Reflection*. Allen, Tex.: Thomas More, 1996.

Navone, John. *Themes of St. Luke*. Rome: Gregorian University Press, 1970.

Neblett, William R. "Forgiveness and Ideals." *Mind* 83 (1974) 269–75.

Newman, Barclay M. and Eugene A. Nida. *A Translator's Handbook on the Acts of the Apostles*. Helps for Translators Series. New York: United Bible Societies, 1972.

Neyrey, Jerome. H. "The Absence of Jesus' Emotions: The Lucan Redaction of Lk 22, 39-46." *Biblica* 61 (1980) 153–71.

_____. *Christ Is Community: The Christologies of the New Testament*. Good News Studies 13. Wilmington, Del.: Michael Glazier, 1985.

_____. *The Passion According to Luke: A Redactional Study of Luke's Soteriology*. New York: Paulist Press, 1985.

Norris, David Amherst. "Forgiving From the Heart: A Biblical and Psychotherapeutic Exploration." Ph.D. diss., Union Theological Seminary, 1983.

O'Brien, P. T. "Prayer in Luke-Acts." *Tyndale Bulletin* 24 (1973) 111–27.

O'Toole, Robert F. "Activity of the Risen Jesus in Luke-Acts." *Biblica* 62 (1981) 471–98.

_____. *The Unity of Luke's Theology: An Analysis of Luke-Acts*. Wilmington, Del.: Michael Glazier, 1984.

Park, Younghee Oh. "The Development of Forgiveness in the Context of Friendship Conflict." Ph.D. diss., University of Wisconsin-Madison, 1989.

Patton, John. *Is Human Forgiveness Possible?: A Pastoral Care Perspective*. Nashville: Abingdon Press, 1985.

Perrin, Norman. *The Kingdom of God in the Teaching of Jesus*. Philadelphia: The Westminster Press, 1963.

Phillips, Lynda J. and John W. Osborne. "Cancer Patients' Experiences of Forgiveness Therapy." *Canadian Journal of Counseling* 23:3 (1989) 236–51.

Pingleton, Jared P. "The Role and Function of Forgiveness in the Psychotherapeutic Process." *Journal of Psychology and Theology* 17:1 (1989) 27–35.

Piper, John. *"Love Your Enemies": Jesus' Love Command in the Synoptic Gospels and the Early Christian Paraenesis*. Society for New Testament Studies Monograph Series 38. Cambridge: Cambridge University Press, 1979.

Plymale, Steven Frederick. "The Prayer Texts of Luke-Acts." Ph.D. diss., Northwestern University, 1986.

Powell, Mark Allan. "The Religious Leaders in Luke: A Literary-Critical Study." *Journal of Biblical Literature* 109:1 (1990) 93–110.

Quinn, Jerome D. "Apostolic Ministry and Apostolic Prayer." *Catholic Biblical Quarterly* 33 (1971) 479–91.

Reicke, B. "Judaeo-Christianity and the Jewish Establishment, A.D. 33–66." In *Jesus and the Politics of His Day*, Ernst Bammel and C.F.D. Moule, eds., 145–52. Cambridge: Cambridge University Press, 1984.

Rhode, Melody Goddard. "Forgiveness, Power, and Empathy." Ph.D. diss., Fuller Theological Seminary, 1990.

Ricoeur, Paul. *The Symbolism of Evil*. Emerson Buchanan, trans. Boston: Beacon Press, 1967.

Robinson, Laura Jo. "The Role of Forgiving in Emotional Healing: A Theological and Psychological Analysis." Ph.D. diss., Fuller Theological Seminary, 1988.

Rooney, Anthony James. "Finding Forgiveness Through Psychotherapy: An Empirical Phenomenological Investigation." Ph.D. diss., Georgia State University, 1989.

Ruether, Rosemary Radford. *Sexism and God-Talk: Toward a Feminist Theology*. Boston: Beacon Press, 1983.

Schmidt, Mellis Irene. "Forgiveness as the Focus Theme in Group Counseling." Ph.D. diss., North Texas State University, 1986.

Schneider, Gerhard. *Die Apostelgeschichte*. Freiburg: Herder, 1980.

Schwager, Raymund. *Must There Be Scapegoats?* Maria L. Assad, trans. San Francisco: Harper and Row, 1987.

Segundo, Juan. *Liberation of Theology*. John Drury, trans. Maryknoll, N.Y.: Orbis Books, 1976.

Senior, Donald. "Jesus in Crisis: The Passion Prayers of Luke's Gospel." In *Scripture and Prayer*, Carolyn Osiek and Donald Senior, eds., 117–30. Wilmington, Del.: Michael Glazier, 1988.

_____. *The Passion of Jesus in the Gospel of Luke*. Wilmington, Del.: Michael Glazier, 1989.

_____. *The Passion of Jesus in the Gospel of Mark*. Wilmington, Del.: Michael Glazier, 1984.

Shontz, Franklin C., and Charlotte Rosenak. "Psychological Theories and the Need for Forgiveness: Assessment and Critique." *Journal of Psychology and Christianity* 7:1 (1988) 23–31.

Smalley, Stephen S. "Spirit, Kingdom and Prayer in Luke-Acts." *Novum Testamentum* 15 (1973) 59–71.

Smedes, Lewis B. *The Art of Forgiving.* New York: Ballantine Books, 1996.

_____. *Forgive and Forget: Healing the Hurts We Don't Deserve.* San Francisco: Harper and Row Publishers, 1984.

Sobrino, Jon. "Latin America: Place of Sin and Place of Forgiveness." Dinah Livingstone, trans. In *Forgiveness,* Casiano Floristán and Christian Duquoc, eds., 45–56. Concilium Religion in the Eighties Series 184:2. Edinburgh: T. & T. Clark Ltd., 1986.

Stanley, David M. *Jesus in Gethsemane: The Early Church Reflects on the Suffering of Jesus.* New York: Paulist Press, 1980.

Sweetland, Dennis M. *Our Journey with Jesus: Discipleship According to Luke-Acts.* Collegeville: The Liturgical Press, 1990.

Talbert, Charles H. "Discipleship in Luke-Acts." In *Discipleship in the New Testament,* Fernando F. Segovia, ed., 62–75. Philadelphia: Fortress Press, 1985.

_____. *Literary Patterns, Theological Themes and the Genre of Luke-Acts.* Society of Biblical Literature Monograph Series 20. Missoula, Mont.: Scholars Press, 1974.

_____. *Luke and the Gnostics: An Examination of the Lucan Purpose.* Nashville, Tenn.: Abingdon Press, 1966.

_____. "Martyrdom in Luke-Acts and the Lukan Social Ethic." In *Political Issues in Luke-Acts,* Richard J. Cassidy and Philip J. Scharper, eds., 99–110. Maryknoll, N.Y.: Orbis Books, 1983.

_____. *Reading Luke: A Literary and Theological Commentary on the Third Gospel.* New York: The Crossroad Publishing Co., 1982.

Tannehill, Robert C. *The Narrative Unity of Luke-Acts: A Literary Interpretation.* Vol. 1, *The Gospel According to Luke.* Philadelphia: Fortress Press, 1986.

_____. *The Narrative Unity of Luke-Acts: A Literary Interpretation.* Vol. 2, *The Acts of the Apostles.* Minneapolis: Fortress Press, 1990.

Taylor, Vincent. *The Text of the New Testament.* London: Macmillian and Company, 1963.

Tracy, David. *The Analogical Imagination: Christian Theology and the Culture of Pluralism.* New York: The Crossroad Publishing Company, 1981.

_____. *Blessed Rage for Order: The New Pluralism in Theology.* New York: The Seabury Press, 1975.

Trites, Allison A. *The New Testament Concept of Witness.* Cambridge: Cambridge University Press, 1977.

_____. "The Prayer Motif in Luke-Acts." In *Perspectives on Luke-Acts,* Charles H. Talbert, ed., 168–86. Danville, Va.: Association of Baptist Professors of Religion, 1978.

Trocmé, Andre. *Jesus and the Nonviolent Revolution.* Michael H. Shank and Marlin E. Miller, trans. Scottdale, Penn.: Herald Press, 1973.

Tyson, Joseph B. *The Death of Jesus in Luke-Acts.* Columbia, S.C.: University of South Carolina Press, 1986.

Udick, William S. "Metanoia as Found in the Acts of the Apostles: Some Inferences and Reflections." *The Bible Today* 28 (1967) 1943–6.

Van Linden, Philip. *The Gospel of Luke and Acts.* Message of Biblical Spirituality Series 10. Wilmington, Del.: Michael Glazier, 1986.

Wade, Susan Helen. "The Development of a Scale to Measure Forgiveness." Ph.D. diss., Fuller Theological Seminary, 1989.

Yates, T. "The Words from the Cross, VII: 'And When Jesus Had Cried with a Loud Voice, He Said, Father into Thy Hands I Commend My Spirit' (Luke xxiii. 46)." *Expository Times* 41 (1929–1930) 427–9.

Zehnle, Richard. "The Salvific Character of Jesus' Death in Lucan Soteriology." *Theological Studies* 30:3 (1969) 420–44.

Notes

1. Introducing the Dialogue Partners

1. *Is Human Forgiveness Possible?: A Pastoral Care Perspective* (Nashville: Abingdon Press, 1985) 17–38.

2. David Augsburger, *Caring Enough To Not Forgive: False Forgiveness* (Ventura, Calif.: Regal Books, 1981) 52.

3. "The Capacity To Forgive: An Object Relations Perspective," *Journal of Religion and Health* 27:4 (1988) 317.

4. Ibid., 314–9.

5. *Forgive and Forget: Healing the Hurts We Don't Deserve* (San Francisco: Harper and Row, 1984) 108–10.

6. "Forgiveness: A Dynamic, Theological and Therapeutic Analysis," *Pastoral Psychology* 31:1 (1982) 40–1.

7. "Problems Encountered When We Forgive One Another," *Journal of Psychology and Christianity* 8:1 (1989) 54.

8. "The Cognitive and Emotive Uses of Forgiveness in the Treatment of Anger," *Psychotherapy* 23:4 (1986) 629–30.

9. *Healing Life's Hurts: Healing Memories Through the Five Stages of Forgiveness* (New York: Paulist Press, 1978) 102–11.

10. *Is Human Forgiveness Possible?*, 73.

11. Ibid., 73, 182–3.

12. *Forgive and Forget*, 21.

13. Ibid., 20–6.

14. "Forgiveness and Recidivism," *Pastoral Psychology* 33:1 (1984) 21.

15. "Problems Encountered When We Forgive One Another," 57–8.

16. *Free and Faithful in Christ: Moral Theology for Priests and Laity,* vol. 2, *The Truth Will Set You Free* (New York: The Seabury Press, 1979) 146.

17. "Forgiveness," *Philosophical Quarterly* 15:59 (1965) 132.

18. "Forgiveness and Ideals," *Mind* 83 (1974) 273–4.

19. *The Symbolism of Evil*, trans. Emerson Buchanan (Boston: Beacon Press, 1967) 278.

20. David Tracy, *The Analogical Imagination: Christian Theology and the Culture of Pluralism* (New York: The Crossroad Publishing Company, 1981) 248–65.

21. *The Scapegoat*, trans. Yvonne Freccero (Baltimore: The Johns Hopkins University Press, 1986), 109.

22. Ibid., 207.

23. Ibid., 211.

24. Ibid., 111. For a biblical testing of Girard's hermeneutic, see Raymund Schwager, *Must There Be Scapegoats?: Violence and Redemption in the Bible*, trans. Maria L. Assad (San Francisco: Harper and Row, 1987). More recently, Gil Bailie's *Violence Unveiled: Humanity at the Crossroads* (New York: Crossroad, 1995) suggests that the weakness of sacrificial systems with their characteristic scapegoats have been exposed by the cross of Jesus Christ. The Gospel proclaims that the Victim who was rejected is Lord. This proclamation brings religious solidarity with victims everywhere.

25. Frank Matera, *Passion Narratives and Gospel Theologies: Interpreting the Synoptics Through Their Passion Stories* (New York: Paulist Press, 1986) 185.

26. Joseph A. Fichtner, "Christ Humiliated and Exalted," *Worship* 36:5 (1962) 313.

27. *The Passion According To Luke: A Redactional Study of Luke's Soteriology* (New York: Paulist Press, 1985) 142–55. See also Brian Beck, "*Imitatio Christi* and the Lucan Passion Narrative," in *Suffering and Martyrdom in the New Testament*, William Horbury and Brian McNeil, eds. (Cambridge: Cambridge University Press, 1981) 46–7.

28. "Latin America: Place of Sin and Place of Forgiveness," in *Forgiveness*, Casiano Floristán and Christian Duquoc, eds. Concilium Religion in the Eighties Series, 184:2 (Edinburgh: T. & T. Clark Ltd., 1986) 45.

29. *The Unity of Luke's Theology: An Analysis of Luke-Acts* (Wilmington, Del.: Michael Glazier, 1984) 86.

30. "*Imitatio Christi* and the Lucan Passion Narrative," 46.

31. For an example of how these dynamics work within the context of a contemporary forgiveness dilemma see my *Why Can't I Forgive You?: A Christian Reflection* (Allen, Tex.: Thomas More, 1996).

32. Joseph A. Fitzmyer, *The Gospel According To Luke I–IX,* Anchor Bible 28 (Garden City, N.Y.: Doubleday and Company, Inc., 1981) 223–4.

33. *Essays in New Testament Interpretation* (Cambridge: Cambridge University Press, 1982) 258.

34. "Jesus in Crisis: The Passion Prayers of Luke's Gospel," *Scripture* and *Prayer,* Carolyn Osiek and Donald Senior, eds. (Wilmington, Del.: Michael Glazier, 1988) 126.

35. *Luke* (Wilmington, Del.: Michael Glazier, Inc., 1980) 277.

36. John Navone, *Themes of St. Luke* (Rome: Gregorian University Press, 1970) 177.

37. G.W.H. Lampe, "The Holy Spirit in the Writings of St. Luke," in *Studies in the Gospels: Essays in Memory of R. H. Lightfoot,* D. E. Nineham, ed. (Oxford: Basil Blackwell, 1967) 159–200.

38. *Apostasy and Perseverance in the Theology of Luke* (Rome: Pontifical Biblical Institute, 1969) 124. For further discussion concerning the ironic use of persecution for the good of the Church in the Lucan corpus, see Charles H. Talbert, *Luke and the Gnostics: An Examination of the Lucan Purpose* (Nashville: Abingdon Press, 1966) 76; and Donald Juel, *Luke-Acts: The Promise of History* (Atlanta: John Knox Press, 1983) 95–100.

39. Fitzmyer, *The Gospel According To Luke I-IX,* 238.

40. Christian Duquoc in "The Forgiveness of God," trans. Oain McGonagle, in *Forgiveness,* Casiano Floristán and Christian Duquoc, eds. Concilium Religion in the Eighties Series, 184:2 (Edinburgh: T. & T. Clark Ltd., 1986) 38.

2. The Context of the Lucan Prayer of Forgiveness

1. Lindell O. Harris, "Prayer in the Gospel of Luke," *Southwestern Journal of Theology* 10:1 (1967) 59–69; P. T. O'Brien, "Prayer in Luke-Acts," *Tyndale Bulletin* 24 (1973) 111–27; Allison A. Trites, "The Prayer Motif in Luke-Acts," in *Perspectives on Luke-Acts,* ed. Charles H. Talbert (Danville, Va.: Association of Baptist Professors of Religion, 1978) 168–86; Harvie M. Conn, "Luke's Theology of Prayer," *Christianity Today* 17:6 (1972) 290–2; Oscar Gerald Harris, "Prayer in Luke-Acts: A Study in the Theology of Luke" (Ph.D. diss., Vanderbilt University, 1966); and Steven Frederick Plymale, "The Prayer Texts of Luke-Acts" (Ph.D. diss., Northwestern University, 1986).

2. O'Brien, "Prayer in Luke-Acts," 113–6.

3. For a fuller development of the theme of prayer in the Acts of the Apostles see Trites, "The Prayer Motif in Luke-Acts," 179–81; and O'Brien, "Prayer in Luke-Acts," 121–7.

4. Fitzmyer, *The Gospel According to Luke I-IX,* 244.

5. Ibid., 245–7.

6. Luke 1:10; 3:21; 5:16; 6:12; 6:28; 9:18; 9:28; 9:29; 11:1 (2 occurrences); 11:2; 18:1; 18:10; 18:11; 20:47; 22:40; 22:41; 22:44; and 22:46.

7. Acts 1:24; 6:6; 8:15; 9:11; 9:40; 10:9; 10:30; 11:5; 12:12; 13:3; 14:23; 16:25; 20:36; 21:5; 22:17; and 28:8.

8. Mark 1:35; 6:46; 11:24; 11:25; 12:40; 13:18; 13:33; 14:32; 14:35; 14:38; and 14:39.

9. Matt 5:44; 6:5 (2 occurrences); 6:6 (2 occurrences); 6:7; 6:9; 14:23; 19:13; 23:14; 24:20; 26:36; 26:39; 26:41; 26:42; and 26:44.

10. Luke 6:12; 19:46; and 22:45.

11. Acts 1:14; 2:42; 3:1; 6:4; 10:4; 10:31; 12:5; 16:13; and 16:16.

12. Matt 17:21; 21:13; and 21:22.

13. Mark 9:29 and 11:17.

14. Statistics obtained from Kurt Aland, *Vollständige Konkordanz zum griechischen Neuen Testament unter Zugrundelegung aller modernen kritischen Textausgaben und des Textus receptus* (Berlin: Walter de Gruyter, 1983) 1176–7.

15. Plymale, "The Prayer Texts of Luke-Acts," 3.

16. O'Brien, "Prayer in Luke-Acts," 113.

17. Harris, "Prayer in Luke-Acts," 16–21.

18. For a study of the importance of prayer in the Gospel of Luke in comparison with the other three gospels see Trites, "The Prayer Motif in Luke-Acts," 170–3; and O'Brien, "Prayer in Luke-Acts," 113–21.

19. Harris, "Prayer in Luke-Acts," 22.

20. Ibid., 197.

21. I. Howard Marshall, *The Gospel of Luke: A Commentary on the Greek Text* (Grand Rapids, Mich.: William B. Eerdmans Publishing Company, 1978) 54–6, 152, 181–2, 198, 210, 237, 362–3, 366, 380–3, 828–33 and 861–8.

22. This is the thesis of Harris, "Prayer in Luke-Acts," 2–3. His thesis is supported by Stephen S. Smalley in "Spirit, Kingdom and Prayer in Luke-Acts," *Novum Testamentum* 15 (1973) 60–1, and Plymale, although Plymale offers refinements to some of Harris' comments, in "The Prayer Texts of Luke-Acts," 11–3.

23. Conn, "Luke's Theology of Prayer," 290–1.

24. Fitzmyer, *The Gospel According to Luke I-IX*, 575–6.

25. O'Brien, "Prayer in Luke-Acts," 111–7.

26. Joachim Jeremias, *The Prayers of Jesus*, trans. John Bowden, Christoph Burchard, and John Reumann (Naperville, Ill.: Alec R. Allenson, Inc., 1967) 76–7.

27. Conn, "Luke's Theology of Prayer," 291.

28. Fitzmyer, *The Gospel According to Luke I-IX*, 247.

29. Since in Mark 3:13, Jesus "went up on the mountain"—a place of prayer—Conn in "Luke's Theology of Prayer," 290, does not, unlike Plummer, consider this prayer passage as unique to Luke. In his analysis, Trites, in "The Prayer Motif in Luke-Acts," agrees with Conn, 172.

30. James Hastings, John Selbie, and John Lambert, eds. *A Dictionary of Christ and the Gospels* (New York: Charles Scribner's Sons, 1908) s.v. "Prayer," by A. Plummer, 391–2.

31. Conn, "Luke's Theology of Prayer," 290.

32. "The Prayer Motif in Luke-Acts," 176.

33. Joseph A. Fitzmyer, *The Gospel According to Luke (X-XXIV)* (Garden City, N.Y.: Doubleday and Company, Inc., 1985) 1503. See also Marshall, *The Gospel of Luke*, 867–8.

34. *The Expositor's Greek Testament*, vol. 1, pt. 1, *The Synoptic Gospels* (London: Hodder and Stoughton, 1912) 639.

35. *The Interpreter's Bible* (New York: Abingdon Press, 1952) vol. 8, *The Gospel According to St. Luke*, 408.

36. Bruce M. Metzger, *A Textual Commentary on the Greek New Testament* (London: United Bible Societies, 1971) 180.

37. Marshall, *The Gospel of Luke*, 868.

38. G.W.H. Lampe, *Peake's Commentary on the Bible* (London: Thomas Nelson and Sons Ltd., 1963) 841.

39. Robert J. Karris, *The New Jerome Biblical Commentary* (Englewood Cliffs, N.J.: Prentice Hall, 1990) 719. For further discussion concerning the textual evidence regarding Luke 23:34, see Vincent Taylor, *The Text of the New Testament* (London: Macmillan and Company, 1963) 94–5; Brooke Westcott and Fenton Hort, *The New Testament in the Original Greek*, vol. 2, appendix (New York: Harper and Brothers, 1882) 67–8; and Matera, *Passion Narratives and Gospel Theologies*, 184.

40. Nestle-Aland, *Novum Testamentum Graece*, 26th ed. (Stuttgart: Deutsche Bibelgesellschaft, 1979) 342.

41. See Matera, *Passion Narratives and Gospel Theologies*, 184. Frederick W. Danker advocates this position in his first commentary, *Jesus and the New Age According to St. Luke: A Commentary on the Third Gospel* (St. Louis: Clayton Publishing House, 1972) 237, but he changes his opinion in his revised edition, *Jesus and the New Age: A Commentary on St. Luke's Gospel* (Philadelphia: Fortress Press, 1988) 373.

42. Robert J. Karris, *What Are They Saying About Luke and Acts?: A Theology of the Faithful God* (New York: Paulist Press, 1979) 49.

43. O'Toole, *The Unity of Luke's Theology*, 23–32.

44. I. Howard Marshall, *Luke: Historian and Theologian* (Grand Rapids, Mich.: Zondervan Publishing House, 1970) 103–6.

45. Ibid., 105–6.

46. Ibid., 106.

47. Can also be translated "(involved) in my Father's affairs" or "among those people belonging to my Father." See Fitzmyer, *The Gospel According to Luke I-IX*, 443.

48. Erich Fascher, "Theologische Beobachtungen zu *dei*" in *Neutestamentliche Studien für Rudolf Bultmann*, W. Eltester, ed. (Berlin: Alfred Töpelmann, 1954) 228–54. See also Charles H. Cosgrove, "The Divine *dei* in Luke-Acts: Investigations into the Lukan Understanding of God's Providence," *Novum Testamentum* 26:2 (1984) 168–90.

49. O'Toole, *The Unity of Luke's Theology*, 26–8.

50. Charles H. Talbert, "Discipleship in Luke-Acts," in *Discipleship in the New Testament*, Fernando F. Segovia, ed. (Philadelphia: Fortress Press, 1985) 62–75; and Robert C. Tannehill, *The Narrative Unity of Luke-Acts: A Literary Interpretation*, vol. 1, *The Gospel According to Luke* (Philadelphia: Fortress Press, 1986) 53–60.

51. For a theological discussion concerning destiny as inherent to vocation, see Leonardo Boff's, *O destino do homen e do mundo: Ensaio sobre a vocação humana* (Petrópolis: Editora Vozes Ltda., 1973) 10–43.

52. *Passion Narratives and Gospel Theologies*, 151.

53. "Luke 23:47 and the Lucan View of Jesus' Death," *Journal of Biblical Literature* 105:1 (1986) 68–70.

54. Matera, *Passion Narratives and Gospel Theologies*, 158.

55. Tannehill, *The Narrative Unity of Luke-Acts*, vol. 1, 43–4 and 68–73.

56. "Luke's Theology of the Death of Jesus," in *Sin, Salvation, and the Spirit*, Daniel Durken, ed. (Collegeville, Minn.: The Liturgical Press, 1979) 228. See also Tannehill, *The Narrative Unity of Luke-Acts*, vol. 1, 282–9; and James M. Dawsey, *The Lucan Voice: Confusion and Irony in the Gospel of Luke* (Macon, Ga.: Mercer University, 1986) 143–56.

57. Robert J. Karris, "Missionary Communities: A New Paradigm for the Study of Luke-Acts," *Catholic Biblical Quarterly* 41 (1979) 84–7; Tyson, *The Death of Jesus in Luke-Acts*, 72–9; G.W.H. Lampe, "'Grievous Wolves' (Acts 20:29)," in *Christ and Spirit in the New Testament*, Barnabas Lindars and Stephen Smalley, eds. (London: Cambridge University Press, 1973) 253–68; B. Reicke, "Judaeo-Christianity and the Jewish Establishment, A.D. 33–66," in *Jesus and the Politics of His Day*, Ernst Bammel and C.F.D. Moule, eds. (Cambridge: Cambridge University Press, 1984) 145–52; and T. D. Barnes, "Legislation Against the Christians," *Journal of Roman Studies* 58 (1968) 32–50.

58. Arland J. Hultgren, "Paul's Pre-Christian Persecutions of the Church: Their Purpose, Locale, and Nature," *Journal of Biblical Literature* 95:1 (1976) 97–111.

59. For an overview of this discussion, see Frank Matera, "Luke 22, 66–71: Jesus Before the Presbyterion," *Ephemerides Theologicae Lovanienses* 65:1 (1989) 43–5.

60. J. Massyngbaerde Ford, "The Seething Cauldron of First-Century Palestine," chap. in *My Enemy Is My Guest: Jesus and Violence in Luke* (Maryknoll, N.Y.: Orbis Books, 1984) 1–12; Andre Trocmé, *Jesus and the Nonviolent Revolution*, trans. Michael H. Shank and Marlin E. Miller (Scottdale, Penn.: Herald Press, 1973) 53–106; and Eduard Lohse, *The New Testament Environment*, trans. John E. Steely (Nashville, Tenn.: Abingdon, 1976) 34–54, 74–120.

61. Helmut Merkel, "The Opposition Between Jesus and Judaism," in *Jesus and the Politics of his Day*, Ernst Bammel and C.F.D. Moule, eds. (Cambridge: Cambridge University Press, 1984) 129–31.

62. *The Narrative Unity of Luke-Acts*, vol. 1, 178–9.

63. Tyson, *The Death of Jesus in Luke-Acts*, 119–29.

64. *Martyrdom and Persecution in the Early Church: A Study of a Conflict from the Maccabees to Donatus* (Garden City, N.Y.: Doubleday and Company, Inc., 1967) 64.

65. Robert Maddox, *The Purpose of Luke-Acts* (Edinburgh: T. & T. Clark, 1982) 82; and Charles H. Talbert in *Literary Patterns, Theological Themes and the Genre of Luke-Acts* (Missoula, Mont.: Scholars Press, 1974) 96–7.

66. Fitzmyer, *The Gospel According to Luke I-IX*, 235–41.

67. Karris, "Luke 23:47 and the Lucan View of Jesus' Death," 67.

68. *The Gospel According to Luke I-IX*, 241–2.

69. Neyrey, *The Passion According to Luke*, 129–55.

70. Trites, "The Prayer Motif in Luke-Acts," 176.

71. Fitzmyer, *The Gospel According to Luke I-IX*, 245.

72. Richard Zehnle, "The Salvific Character of Jesus' Death in Lucan Soteriology," *Theological Studies* 30:3 (1969) 443.

73. Brown, *Apostasy and Perseverance in the Theology of Luke*, 7–10. Susan R. Darrett, *The Demise of the Devil: Magic and the Demonic in Luke's Writings* (Minneapolis: Fortress Press, 1989) 46–54.

74. Danker, *Jesus and the New Age* (1988) 378–9; and Robert J. Karris, *Luke: Artist and Theologian: Luke's Passion Account As Literature* (New York: Paulist Press, 1985) 106.

75. *The Theology of St. Luke* (New York: Harper and Row, Publishers, 1960) 16.

76. *Apostasy and Perseverance in the Theology of Luke*, 7.

77. "A Note on Luke xxii 36," *Novum Testamentum* 7 (1964) 133.

78. Ibid.

79. *My Enemy Is My Guest*, 116.

80. *The Passion According to Luke*, 43.

81. *Passion Narratives and Gospel Theologies*, 166.

82. Ibid., 157–8.

83. Ibid., 158.

84. Brown, *Apostasy and Perseverance in the Theology of Luke*, 12–9.

85. Jerome H. Neyrey, "The Absence of Jesus' Emotions: The Lucan Redaction of Luke 22, 39-46," *Biblica* 61 (1980) 171.

86. David M. Stanley, *Jesus in Gethsemane: The Early Church Reflects on the Suffering of Jesus* (New York: Paulist Press, 1980) 212–3.

87. Ibid., 213

88. Matera, *Passion Narratives and Gospel Theologies*, 169.

89. Ibid., 171.

90. O'Toole, *The Unity of Luke's Theology*, 136–7.

91. Barclary M. Newman and Eugene A. Nida, *A Translator's Handbook on the Acts of the Apostles* (New York: United Bible Societies, 1972) 142; and Richard J. Cassidy, *Society and Politics in the Acts of the Apostles* (Maryknoll, N.Y.: Orbis Books, 1987) 34–6.

92. Allison A. Trites in *The New Testament Concept of Witness* (Cambridge: Cambridge University Press, 1977) 132.

93. Dennis M. Sweetland, *Our Journey with Jesus: Discipleship According to Luke-Acts* (Collegeville, Minn.: The Liturgical Press, 1990) 100–1.

94. Cassidy, *Society and Politics in the Acts of the Apostles*, 36–8. For a critique of Cassidy's portrayal of Lucan nonviolence, see Talbert, "Martyrdom in Luke-Acts and the Lukan Social Ethic," 106–9.

95. O'Toole, "The Disciples Continue the Work of Jesus" in *The Unity of Luke's Theology*, 62–94; Robert C. Tannehill, *The Narrative Unity of Luke-Acts: A Literary Interpretation*, vol. 2, *The Acts of the Apostles* (Minneapolis: Fortress Press, 1990) 99–101; and Talbert, "Martyrdom in Luke-Acts and the Lukan Social Ethic," 100.

96. Matera in *Passion Narratives and Gospel Theologies* insists that "Luke portrays Jesus as the Messiah who refuses to save himself, but continues to save others even at the moment of death," 186.

97. Charles H. Talbert, *Reading Luke: A Literary and Theological Commentary on the Third Gospel* (New York: Crossroad Publishing Co., 1982) 212–8; and Beck, "*Imitatio Christi* and the Lucan Passion Narrative," 28–47.

3. The Process of the Lucan Prayer of Forgiveness

1. Plymale, "The Prayer Texts of Luke-Acts," 190.

2. Donald Senior, *The Passion of Jesus in the Gospel of Luke* (Wilmington, Del.: Michael Glazier, 1989) 167–9.

3. Sweetland, *Our Journey with Jesus*, 116–8.

4. Ibid., 125–6.

5. For an illustration of the contrast of Jesus' death and the deaths of the Maccabean martyrs, see Ford, *My Enemy Is My Guest*, 131.

6. F. F. Bruce, *The Book of Acts* (Grand Rapids, Mich.: William B. Eerdmans Publishing Company, 1988) 160.

7. See Elisabeth Schüssler Fiorenza's presidential address to the Society of Biblical Literature, "The Ethics of Biblical Interpretation: Decentering Biblical Scholarship," *Journal of Biblical Literature* 107 (1988) 3–17.

8. Jeremias, *The Prayers of Jesus*, 12.

9. Ibid., 13.

10. Navone, *Themes of St. Luke*, 52–3.

11. Jacques Dupont, "Conversion in the Acts of the Apostles," chap. in *The Salvation of the Gentiles: Studies in the Acts of the Apostles*, trans. John R. Keating (New York: Paulist Press, 1979) 61–84; Francis X. Hezel, "'Conversion' and 'Repentance' in Lucan Theology," *The Bible Today* 37 (1968) 2596–602; and William S. Udick, "Metanoia as Found in the Acts of the Apostles: Some Inferences and Reflections," *The Bible Today* 28 (1967) 1943–6.

12. Raymond E. Brown, "The Pater Noster as an Eschatological Prayer," *Theological Studies* 22:2 (1961) 183–5.

13. Senior, *The Passion of Jesus in the Gospel of Luke,* 129.

14. Tannehill, *The Narrative Unity of Luke-Acts,* vol. 1, 65.

15. Ibid., 103–4.

16. Fitzmyer, *The Gospel According to Luke I-IX,* 579–80.

17. Tannehill, *The Narrative Unity of Luke-Acts,* vol. 1, 103–9.

18. Senior, *The Passion of Jesus in the Gospel of Luke,* 136–8; and Jerome H. Neyrey, *Christ Is Community: The Christologies of the New Testament* (Wilmington, Del.: Michael Glazier, 1985) 114–5.

19. Neyrey, *Christ Is Community,* 116–8.

20. Trites, "The Prayer Motif in Luke-Acts," 175.

21. See *Theological Dictionary of the New Testament,* s.v. *aphiemi,* vol. 1, 512.

22. Plymale, "The Prayer Texts of Luke-Acts," 139.

23. D. Daube, "'For They Know Not What They Do:' Luke 23,34," *Studia Patristica* IV (1961) 69.

24. John M. Creed, *The Gospel According to St. Luke* (London: Macmillan, 1930) 286; and Ford, *My Enemy Is My Guest,* 132–3.

25. Conzelmann, *The Theology of St. Luke,* 89–90.

26. Mark Allan Powell, "The Religious Leaders in Luke: A Literary-Critical Study," *Journal of Biblical Literature* 109:1 (1990) 93–110.

27. Daube, "For They Know Not What They Do," 60.

28. Ibid., 61–2.

29. René Girard, *The Scapegoat,* 8.

30. J. Massyngbaerde Ford, "Reconciliation and Forgiveness in Luke's Gospel," in *Political Issues in Luke-Acts,* Richard J. Cassidy and Philip J. Scharper, eds. (Maryknoll, N.Y.: Orbis Books, 1983) 95.

31. *The Theology of St. Luke,* 93.

32. Ford, *My Enemy Is My Guest,* 132.

33. Plymale, "The Prayer Texts of Luke-Acts," 140.

34. "The Laos at the Cross: Luke's Crucifixion Scene," in *The Language of the Cross,* Aelred Lacomara, ed. (Chicago: Franciscan Herald Press, 1977) 77–99.

35. Plymale, "The Prayer Texts of Luke-Acts," 143–4.

36. Ibid., 109–10.

37. Karris, *Luke: Artist and Theologian,* 97.

38. Senior, in *The Passion of Jesus in the Gospel of Luke*, argues that the addressing of the psalm to the Father is "the only significant change the evangelist has made in citing the Psalm," 143. Frank Matera, however, sees both the direct address as well as the verb change as significant. See "The Death of Jesus According to Luke: A Question of Sources," *Catholic Biblical Quarterly* 47 (1985) 476–7.

39. Donald Senior, *The Passion of Jesus in the Gospel of Mark* (Wilmington, Del.: Michael Glazier, 1984) 123–6.

40. For an analysis of the allusions to the lament Psalms in the Lucan passion prayers see Darrell L. Bock, *Proclamation From Prophecy and Pattern: Lucan Old Testament Christology. Journal for the Study of the New Testament Supplement Series*, 12 (Sheffield, England: Sheffield Academic Press, 1987) 143–8.

41. Danker, *Jesus and the New Age* (1988) 381.

42. "The Death of Jesus According to Luke," 475–7.

43. Ibid.

44. I am grateful to M. Dennis Hamm, S.J., of Creighton University for this insight.

45. Fitzmyer, *The Gospel According to Luke I-IX*, 224–5.

46. Senior, *The Passion of Jesus in the Gospel of Luke*, 144–5.

47. Xavier Léon-Dufour, *Life and Death in the New Testament: The Teachings of Jesus and Paul*, trans. Terrence Prendergast (San Francisco: Harper and Row Publishers, 1986) 131–3.

48. G.W.H. Lampe, *God As Spirit*, The Bampton Lectures, 1976 (Oxford: Clarendon Press, 1977) 162.

49. Bock, *Proclamation From Prophecy and Pattern*, 225.

50. Plymale, "The Prayer Texts of Luke-Acts," 186.

51. Gerhard Schneider, *Die Apostelgeschichte* (Freiburg: Herder, 1980) 477.

52. Hermann L. Strack and Paul Billerbeck, *Kommentar zum Neuen Testament aus Talmud und Midrasch*, vol. 2 (München: C. H. Becksche Verlagsbuchhandlung, 1924) 269; Trites, "The Prayer Motif in Luke-Acts," 173; and Gustaf Dalman, *Jesus-Jeshua: Studies in the Gospels*, trans. Paul P. Levertoff (London: S.P.C.K. 1929; repr., New York: KTAV Publishing House, Inc., 1971) 210.

53. *Proclamation From Prophecy and Pattern*, 147.

54. Plymale, "The Prayer Texts of Luke-Acts," 142–4.

55. Neyrey, *The Passion According to Luke*, 142–3.

56. Ibid., 142–54.

57. *The Gospel of Luke* (Greenwood, S.C.: The Attic Press, Inc., 1974) 270.

58. For a further discussion, see Crowe, "The Laos at the Cross," 90–3.

59. Plymale, "The Prayer Texts of Luke-Acts," 140.

60. Brown, *Perseverance in the Theology of Luke*, 19.

61. Plymale, "The Prayer Texts of Luke-Acts," 174–83.

62. Robert O'Toole, "Activity of the Risen Jesus in Luke-Acts," *Biblica* 62 (1981) 480–2.

63. Frend, *Martyrdom and Persecution in the Early Church*, 114–5.

64. Zehnle, "The Salvific Character of Jesus' Death in Lucan Soteriology," 430.

65. Senior, *The Passion of Jesus in the Gospel of Luke*, 168.

66. *The Kingdom of God in the Teaching of Jesus* (Philadelphia: The Westminster Press, 1963) 185–201.

67. *Response to the End of History: Eschatology and Situation in Luke-Acts*, SBL Dissertation Series 92 (Atlanta, Ga.: Scholars Press, 1988) 18.

68. Eric Franklin, *Christ the Lord: A Study in the Purpose and Theology of Luke-Acts* (Philadelphia: The Westminster Press, 1975) 60–1.

69. Carroll, *Response to the End of History*, 165–7.

70. Franklin, *Christ the Lord*, 94.

71. G.W.H. Lampe, "Martyrdom and Inspiration," in *Suffering and Martyrdom in the New Testament*, William Horbury and Brian McNeil, eds. (Cambridge: Cambridge University Press, 1981) 129–32.

72. Plymale, "The Prayer Texts of Luke-Acts," 190.

73. Joel B. Green, "The Death of Jesus, God's Servant," in *Reimaging the Death of the Lukan Jesus*, Dennis D. Sylva, ed., *Athenäums Monografien, Bonner Biblische Beiträge* 73 (Frankfurt: Hain, 1990) 8–10. See also O'Toole, *The Unity of Luke's Theology*, 51, 237.

74. John Piper, *"Love Your Enemies": Jesus' Love Command in the Synoptic Gospels and the Early Christian Paraenesis*, Society for New Testament Studies Monograph Series, 28 (Cambridge: Cambridge University Press, 1979) 173.

75. Trites, "The Prayer Motif in Luke-Acts," 174–9.

76. Ibid., 179–84.

77. Lampe, "The Holy Spirit in the Writings of St. Luke," 169.

78. Harris, "Prayer in Luke-Acts," 240.

79. Lampe, "The Holy Spirit in the Writings of St. Luke," 169–71.

80. Ibid., 184–7.

81. Ibid., 67–71.

4. Answering Real Questions:
The Contribution of Pastoral Theology

1. See for example T. L. Brink, "The Role of Religion in Later Life: A Case of Consolation and Forgiveness," *Journal of Psychology and Christianity* 4:2 (1985) 22–5; Beverly J. Flanigan, "Shame and Forgiving in Alcoholism," *Alcoholism Treatment Quarterly* 4:2 (1987) 181–95; Lynda J. Phillips and John W. Osborne, "Cancer Patients' Experiences of Forgiveness Therapy," *Canadian Journal of Counselling* 23:3 (1989) 236–51; Younghee Oh Park, "The Development of Forgiveness in the Context of Friendship Conflict" (Ph.D. diss., The University of Wisconsin-Madison, 1989); Radhi Hasan Al-Mabuk, "The Commitment to Forgive in Parentally Love-Deprived College Students" (Ph.D. diss., The University of Wisconsin-Madison, 1990); and John Howard Hebl, "Forgiveness as a Counseling Goal with Elderly Females" (Ph.D. diss., The University of Wisconsin-Madison, 1990).

2. See Jeffrey M. Brandsma, "Forgiveness: A Dynamic, Theological and Therapeutic Analysis," 40–50; Richard P. Fitzgibbons, "The Cognitive and Emotive Uses of Forgiveness in the Treatment of Anger," 629–33; John Gartner, "The Capacity to Forgive: An Object Relations Perspective," 313–20; Jared P. Pingleton, "The Role and Function of Forgiveness in the Psychotherapeutic Process," *Journal of Psychology and Theology* 17:1 (1989) 27–35; Anthony James Rooney, "Finding Forgiveness Through Psychotherapy: An Empirical Phenomenological Investigation" (Ph.D. diss., Georgia State University, 1989) etc.

3. For an analysis of psychological literature illustrating this claim, see Susan H. Wade, "The Development of a Scale to Measure Forgiveness" (Ph.D. diss., Fuller Theological Seminary, 1989) 29–51.

4. These works are cited in studies that are primarily psychological in tone: i.e., Pingleton in "The Role and Function of Forgiveness in the Psychotherapeutic Process" cites Augsburger, the Linns, and Smedes; Fitzgibbons in "The Cognitive and Emotive Uses of Forgiveness in the Treatment of Anger" cites Smedes; Enright and Zell in "Problems Encountered When We Forgive One Another" cite Augsburger, the Linns and Smedes; Robert Enright, Maria Santos, and Radhi Al-Mabuk in "The Adolescent as Forgiver," *Journal of Adolescence* 12:1 (1989) cite the Linns and Smedes; Nathaniel Curtis in "The

Structure and Dynamics of Forgiving Another" (Ph.D. diss., United States International University, 1986) cites Augsburger, the Linns, and Smedes; David Michael Droll in "Forgiveness: Theory and Research" (Ph.D. diss., University of Nevada, 1984), cites Augsburger; Rooney in "Finding Forgiveness Through Psychotherapy: An Empirical Phenomenological Investigation," cites the Linns, Patton, and Smedes; Neil Robert Fow in "An Empirical-Phenomenological Investigation of the Experience of Forgiving Another" (Ph.D. diss., University of Pittsburgh) cites Smedes; Hebl in "Forgiveness as a Counseling Goal with Elderly Females" cites Augsburger, Patton, and Smedes; Park in "The Development of Forgiveness in the Context of Friendship Conflict" cites Donnelly, Patton, and Smedes; Al-Mabuk in "The Commitment to Forgive in Parentally Love-Deprived College Students" cites Smedes; Mellis Irene Schmidt in "Forgiveness as the Focus Theme in Group Counseling" (Ph.D. diss., North Texas State University, 1986) cites Augsburger; David Eastin in "The Treatment of Adult Female Incest Survivors by Psychological Forgiveness Processes" (Ph.D. diss., The University of Wisconsin-Madison, 1989) cites Augsburger, Donnelly, the Linns, Patton, and Smedes—or in works that are more pastoral in tone: i.e., Laura Jo Robinson in "The Role of Forgiving in Emotional Healing: A Theological and Psychological Analysis" (Ph.D. diss., Fuller Theological Seminary, 1988) cites Augsburger, Donnelly, the Linns, Patton, and Smedes; Donald Hope in "The Healing Paradox of Forgiveness," *Psychotherapy* 24:2 (1987) cites Donnelly.

5. Augsburger, *Caring Enough To Forgive*, 32.

6. Ibid., 37–8.

7. Augsburger, *Caring Enough To Not Forgive*, 69.

8. Ibid., 70.

9. Doris Donnelly, *Learning To Forgive* (Nashville, Tenn.: Abingdon Press, 1979) 2–3. Donnelly suggests a process for the identification of hurts in *Putting Forgiveness Into Practice* (Allen, Tex.: Argus Communications, 1982) 1–7.

10. Donnelly, *Learning to Forgive*, 84–99.

11. Linn and Linn, *Healing Life's Hurts*, 1–7.

12. Elizabeth Kübler-Ross, *On Death and Dying* (New York: Macmillan) 1969.

13. Linn and Linn, *Healing Life's Hurts*, 8–17.

14. Patton, *Is Human Forgiveness Possible?*, 16.

15. Ibid., 178–82.

16. Ibid., 16.

17. Ibid., 186.
18. Smedes, *Forgive and Forget*, 94.
19. Ibid., 134–51.
20. Augsburger, *Caring Enough to Not Forgive*, 8.
21. Ibid., 26.
22. Donnelly, *Learning to Forgive*, 2–3.
23. Linn and Linn, *Healing Life's Hurts*, 9.
24. Ibid., 34–48.
25. Patton, *Is Human Forgiveness Possible?*, 141.
26. Ibid., 65–7.
27. Ibid., 16.
28. Ibid.
29. Smedes, *Forgive and Forget*, 38–49.
30. Ibid., 108.
31. Augsburger, *Caring Enough To Not Forgive*, 70–3.
32. Donnelly, *Learning to Forgive*, 62–5.
33. Linn and Linn, *Healing Life's Hurts*, 1–7.
34. Patton, *Is Human Forgiveness Possible?*, 36.
35. Ibid., 117–45.
36. Ibid., 16.
37. Ibid., 148.
38. Smedes, *Forgive and Forget*, 124.
39. Ibid., 129–32.
40. Augsburger, *Caring Enough To Forgive*, 13.
41. Ibid., 31.
42. Ibid., 69.
43. Ibid., 69–74.
44. Ibid., 69.
45. Donnelly, *Learning to Forgive*, 66–71.
46. Ibid., 115–9.
47. Linn and Linn, *Healing Life's Hurts*, 8–18.
48. Ibid., 93-101; 111-7; 128-33; 152-63; 173-6; 210.
49. Patton, *Is Human Forgiveness Possible?*, 67–74.
50. Ibid., 147–8.
51. Smedes, *Forgive and Forget*, 136.
52. Ibid.

53. Ibid., 147–51.

54. The Ignatian influence upon the Linns is implicit in their Jesuit training and is also referred to explicitly in the text; e.g., Linn and Linn, *Healing Life's Hurts*, 18; 56–7; 147–8.

55. In *The Spiritual Exercises* Ignatius speaks of the necessity of asking for the grace one desires [48].

56. Augsburger, *Caring Enough To Not Forgive*, 69–70.

57. Augsburger, *Caring Enough To Forgive*, 37–8.

58. Augsburger, *Caring Enough To Not Forgive*, 69–73.

59. Donnelly, *Learning to Forgive*, 2–3.

60. Ibid., 84–99.

61. Linn and Linn, *Healing Life's Hurts*, 1–7.

62. Ibid., 187–8.

63. Patton, *Is Human Forgiveness Possible?*, 165.

64. Ibid., 16.

65. Ibid., 179.

66. Smedes, *Forgive and Forget*, 70.

67. Ibid., 106–7.

68. Ibid., 147–51.

5. Toward a Contemporary Theology of Forgiveness: A Scriptural/Pastoral Dialogue

1. Augsburger, *Caring Enough To Forgive*, 6–7.

2. Donnelly, *Learning To Forgive*, 85–6.

3. Linn and Linn, *Healing Life's Hurts*, 2.

4. Patton, *Is Human Forgiveness Possible?*, 14–5.

5. Ibid., 11.

6. Ibid., 15–6.

7. Smedes, *Forgive and Forget*, 152.

8. Donnelly, *Learning To Forgive*, 84–92.

9. Smedes, *Forgive and Forget*, 124.

10. Patton, *Is Human Forgiveness Possible?*, 16.

11. Augsburger, *Caring Enough to Not Forgive*, 71.

12. Augsburger, *Caring Enough to Forgive*, 13.

13. Ibid., 20.

14. Ibid., 72.

15. Augsburger, *Caring Enough to Not Forgive*, 71–3.

16. Donnelly, *Learning to Forgive*, 67.

17. Linn and Linn, *Healing Life's Hurts*, 17.

18. Patton, *Is Human Forgiveness Possible?*, 16.

19. Smedes, *Forgive and Forget*, 2–5.

20. Ibid., 20–5.

21. Augsburger, *Caring Enough to Not Forgive*, 69–70.

22. Linn and Linn, *Healing Life's Hurts*, 1–7.

23. Patton, *Is Human Forgiveness Possible?*, 16.

24. Smedes, *Forgive and Forget*, 136–7.